The Forty

The Forty Effin Niners

The Adventures of a Part-Time
Security Guard during the Reign
of the Team of the Eighties

Rick Pucci

Library of Congress Control Number: 2018909068
ISBN: Hardcover   978-1-9845-4354-7
                   Softcover   978-1-9845-4353-0
                   eBook   978-1-9845-4352-3

Rev. date: 11/02/2018

To order additional copies of this book, contact:
Xlibris
1-888-795-4274
www.Xlibris.com
Orders@Xlibris.com
781292

PROLOGUE

S O THIS IS how I'm going to die. I always wondered how I'd die. Now I know.

We were under attack. "Look out!" Gunner, the guard behind me, shoved my back.

Good thing too. Another battery whizzed past my ear. Damn. Close call. One of them hits my head, I'm a goner.

Run for cover. We can't. We're doomed. The bent-over guard in front of me was not even moving. Besides, our orders were clear: "Stay in a line behind the police shields." Our boss assigned each guard to one player. But the line's stopped moving. We're sitting ducks.

A smashing sound against a policeman's shield. "Holy shit! What's that ahead on the ground? Is that blood?"

"No, idiot. Someone threw a ketchup bottle. Get this line movin'." Gunner's voice felt panicky. You could smell fear in the air, metallic, slightly musky.

The skies opened. It rained harder than a cow pissing on a flat rock. A head of lettuce smacked the head directly in front of me. The player dropped to a knee. *Jesus.* I looked toward the angry mob. "Where the hell they keep getting all this stuff?"

The rabble-rousers yelled, "Rotten SCABs! Keep out of our stadium!"

"We're taking heavy fire. Stay calm!" I yelled down the line, trying to shrink my body to fit behind the cop's see-through shield between the vitriol-filled mob and me.

The protesters chanted in unison: "SCAB players, turn around, no union busting in this town! SCAB players, turn around!"

"Simply get the strikebreaking replacement players from the NFL busses safely into Candlestick Park," I mimicked my boss's voice aloud while wiping water from my eyes. "Simple, right? But through the very heart of a badass protest?"

I yelled over my right shoulder to Gunner, "Maybe we can retreat back to the bus!"

I spun around and looked at the bus we just departed. Two 300-pound African Americans, current NFL players, wearing camo, obviously royally pissed off at the union-busting replacement players, walked from the front of the bus to the rear, simultaneously smashing every window with their fists. From deep inside the bowels of the bus, female screams emitted intermittently with the sounds of breaking glass.

Okay, probably not a good idea.

"Never mind, Gunner. Retreating is no longer an option."

The replacement player got back up. He rubbed his lettuce-stricken cranium. When another battery whizzed by, he said, "Fuck this," broke rank, and bolted for cover. Damn. My fellow guards followed suit, running for their lives. Debris followed them like hungry locusts.

"Wait !" Goddammit. My job assignment had been simple: keep everyone together behind the cop's shields. But I was too busy saving my own ass. *What the? What the hell are the cops doing? They're pulling back? I thought more were coming. You kidding me? God.*

Exposed, feeling naked, I took off. Running and splashing through the newly formed puddles with black dress shoes sucked. The brass should let us wear sneakers if they're going to have us scurrying around like this. These fans hated us. Run. The showering incoming bombs and rain became one.

I nicknamed my boss *El Capitán*, and it stuck. He and his brass at Gate E waved their arms frantically like those giant blow-up nylon men at the car dealers. "C'mon, move it!" they yelled.

Now, like an ancient warrior of ole leaving the field of battle, I retreated for the sanctuary of Fort Candlestick before the angry Huns could slaughter me. I darted toward the heavy castle door through the arrow-filled air, grabbing my player's arm along the way. The Candlestick drainage flowed before us. We jumped over the alligator-filled moat and made it through the gate—alive.

After ushering the scared-to-death recent bartenders, insurance salesmen, warehouse managers, and handymen—all former football players who overnight became SCABs—to their locker room, we, the soaked guards of Burns Security, huddled to catch our collective breaths. Huffing and puffing, we high-fived one another and watched my fellow fans enter the heavily guarded main entrance, getting overly strip-searched along the way. *Jesus.* Even the paying fans were getting the rough treatment. Security had bent one guy over and appeared to be administering a deep anal probe. Yeah, he'll be buying another season ticket next year after this positive experience.

Outside Candlestick Park's walls of protection, the death chants continued. The horrific smell of something evil burning scorched the nostrils. *Rubber?*

Two guards, brothers, handed the lieutenant their badges. "Fuck this noise. We quit. We felt batteries zipping by our ears."

Another, a rookie, hippy kind of guy, said, "Whoa, dude, I'm so out of here. This is just a part-time job, man. Who needs it?"

"C'mon, guys. Stick it out. This strike'll end in a few weeks," I pleaded. "Weren't we just in the Super Bowl one lousy year ago?"

"Dude, this strike'll wipe out the whole season. Who needs it? Besides, how the hell did we ever end up on the side against the real players? We quit."

The lieutenant now holding the three retired badges spotted me. "*El Capitán* wants to see you now."

Damn. I let out a chestful of air. I failed at my simple job: keeping the line behind those police-escorted shields together at all costs. Now I'll get whacked. I sat and poured water out of my wingtips, which were ruined. I got up and sighed deeply. Soaked to the gills, right down to my tightie-whities, I took the escalator up to get shit-canned.

CHAPTER 1

'80: DAVIS AND SCHOCK

1980 ARRIVED RIGHT on time. The decade of the '80s crashed upon us like the Pacific waves slamming against Cliff Side's rocks. Cruising Route 80, doing eighty miles per hour, I spotted the sign: "Davis 80" as in miles.

I said, "Well, at this speed, by my calculations, we'll be there in one hour."

Looking over at my pal, Van, at the wheel, wearing his red-handkerchief headband, waist-length hair flowing out the noisy window, I asked, "Who's hosting this party again?"

Van, shirtless, grinning as if he were on to something, answered, "Davis."

"Yeah, I know we're going to Davis, just saw the sign, but who's throwing the party?"

I turned down *Led Zeppelin IV* blasting through the sound system in his Aston Martin so he could hear me.

"Davis!" he yelled.

"That's where we're going. Who's on third base?"

He scrunched his face. "What?"

"What's at second?"

"What are you talking about?"

"Said the dry-humored man who somehow never heard Abbott and Costello's schtick."

I continued, "Oh, was Davis also his name? Davis in Davis was throwing the party?"

"Yeah." Van turned the tunes back up, wagged his head, finished the Coors formerly nestled between his cutoff shorts, and fired the bottle out the window.

"Argh. Littering, my pet peeve."

Van said, "Mark Davis. He's cool—one of us. Graduated from high school same time we did, so the dude's in his early twenties too."

"He's related to Al Davis, owner of the Oakland Raiders, right?"

"Yeah, his son, but don't worry about that. He's not all big-headed about it. Your ol' lady's cool with you leaving her behind for this blowout?"

"Joanne? Yeah, she's cool with it. I'm not hen-pecked like you."

Van smiled. We all knew Leslie let him hang with the boys.

I continued, "Joanne knows she's a Sunday football widow."

He said nothing, so I continued. "Ya know, when you think about it, football's the universal language."

"Whad'ya mean?" Van fired up a Marlboro and offered me one as usual. Even though he knows I despise cigarettes as much as I hate littering. He does this just to sharpen his main skill set, being annoying.

"I mean you could drop me off from the stratosphere over America in a parachute," I said. "No matter what city I land in, I simply figure out the closest NFL or college football team and have something in common with any guy in the area."

"Or any chick. Girls dig the game nowadays too, ya know. There'll be a ton of them at this party. So try not to embarrass me."

"Isn't it wild that you and I came from such a small rural coal town back east, Nanticoke-fucking-Pennsylvania? Then you relocate to Piedmont right outside of Oakland. Before, to me, you just lived in *California*.

"Then Joanne and I, as we dreamed of doing throughout those horrible, bone-chilling winters, graduated from Penn State and *boom*, we cruised here to the Bay Area. Joanne, graduated *summa cum laude* and scored a fine hiring package from Texas Instruments. I scraped by and found a job in finance, HFC, while going to grad school only to find you lived right up the friggin' Nimitz freeway. What were the odds?"

"Yeah, and you owe me big time for introducing you to all my friends: Resor, Mikkelson, and Scharbach. I still can't believe you drove cross-country in that piece of shit."

"Excuse me, Mr. Trust Fund Baby. You're speaking of the Beige Mermaid, my Ford LTD, with nylon interior, hideaway headlights, and a V-8 engine. Bought her for $250, drove her cross-country into Canada then Mexico and sold her for $250. That, good sir, was no mere car. That machine was legendary."

The party was phenomenal. Eight kegs of beer and all sorts of debauchery. Mark Davis was attending California State University in Chico. I was in the graduate program at San Jose State University, so we had that in common, but we mainly talked football.

Mark, at his kitchen table, said, "There are two types of fans. I consider you an insider fan. You played four years of high school ball. One and a half years at the collegiate level. You enjoy discussing the inside-the-game stuff, strategy like my dad."

"Okay," I replied.

Mark called his friend over and introduced us. "On the other hand, Jim Schock here"—he threw a headlock around Schock's bearded head— "is more of the external fan. Knows and loves the game too, but he wears it on his sleeve. For Schock, it's life or death. He's more of the roar-of-the-crowd kinda fan, right, Jimmy?" He scraped his knuckles over Jim's head back and forth while Jim brayed.

Jim Schock, dressed in silver and black for the party, nonstop black curly barbed wire hair from his nose on down to the bottom of a beard, a pirate-looking fella, demented, broke free of Mark's grip, bent over the table, snorted a railer, chugged his entire beer, and led the room in a chant, "Let's-go-Ray-Duz."

Son of prominent physician Doc Schock, Jim scored tickets from Mark for every Raiders game. However, his friends often flaked out at the last minute, sticking him with extra seats. Many football fans were and are bandwagon fans. They only follow their teams when they're doing well unlike true fans. How can you appreciate the rainbow if you never walk through the rain? The Raiders were in the rain and not winning. They finished 1978 and 1979 just one game over .500 and a lousy team, the Seattle Seahawks, hammered them in their final home game.

With legendary, bigger-than-life Coach John Madden retiring, Raider Nation went into mourning. They groaned when owner Al Davis handed the reins of the team to quiet, demure Tom Flores. Flores currently had the 1980 Raiders at a paltry 2–3, heading nowhere fast, and the "fans" were jumping off.

My phone rang so loud it shook the lampshade.

It was Jim Schock. "Hey, Rick, remember that party in Davis when you asked, 'If you ever have an extra ticket, give me a buzz'? I have an extra to see the Raiders. You want in?"

"Hell yeah. Let me grab my calendar. It's this month?"

Back East, my God, you'd plan for an NFL game months in advance then take a two-hour Martz bus trip to New York City to see the Giants. You'd buy the package: third deck seating, hoagies, and access to two kegs of beer, one in the front and the other in the back of the bus. The ride home promised to be gross because guys would get too wasted and start projectile-vomiting into the bus's aisles where you eventually had to walk the gauntlet. I shuddered at the memory.

"So, when's the game?" I asked, armed with a pencil and an open calendar.

"Uh, well . . . it started ten minutes ago."

"Jesus. Wow . . . uh . . . okay . . . What the hell . . . Sure, no problem."

I figured by showing I was always available no matter what, I'd continue getting these types of calls. I hung up, kissed Joanne goodbye, and trusted she'd understand. She's the best. We were in love. Then I dashed outside, jumped over the door into my new copper-colored two-seat Fiat Spyder convertible and flew up the Nimitz Highway 17. Got to the Oakland Coliseum in no time flat, parking the Spyder alongside the freeway. Not one other car parked there. After sprinting across the two-hundred-yard green field, I snatched my ticket at will-call and still caught the last three quarters, including Kenny-time. That's the time at the end of each game when Kenny Stabler finally woke up, passed to a wide-open Freddie Biletnikoff, Dave Casper, or Cliff Branch and won the game in dramatic fashion. Always.

After the game, I used my entire arm to sweep away the tickets covering my windshield—a small price to pay to see great NFL action live. Keeping my car registered back East meant I never had to pay them anyway.

This guy Schock was quite a distance over the rainbow if you know what I mean. Much more than just a true "external fan," for each game he'd completely dress in silver-n'-black Raiders regalia, including skintight black spandex pants and the official black Raiders T-shirt. He even had the one bad eye from an accident like the Raiders' logo.

Jim was great to go with to the games, and we hit them all. He provided more entertainment than the games themselves. The Bud beer vendor would sit right beside him. My eyes could not widen any further when I watched Jim slamming those Buds home during the excitement like a machine, one in each hand. He would get our entire section foaming at the mouth yelling along to his frenzied cheers.

One game, he spontaneously created a new cheer, "Let's Say Oakland." Not only did our section get in on it, but the entire Oakland Colesium joined the chant. Rookie Todd Christensen, waiting on the line as part of the suicide squad during the commercial timeout got such a charge out of it, he began waving at us with his huge forearm pad. The kickoff commenced. Todd sprinted downfield, smashed into the ball carrier, recovered the fumble and ran it in for a touchdown. Our section went ballistic when Todd acknowledged us after his score, shaking the football towards us. Astonishing.

At one game, in particular, Schock screamed so loudly, pressed against the pipes in front of our rowdy mezzanine section, leading cheers against the San Diego Chargers of Air Coryell/ Dan Fouts fame, that you literally heard his windpipe crack. His voice was never the same. It often slips in mid-word during his many rambles to this day. I can do a killer Schock imitation. Van and our friends at home watching that game on TV swore they heard Schock's voice above the rabble.

Well, I like to think I brought Oakland good luck. They immediately went from hapless losers to losing only one more game the remainder of the season, to the hated Dallas Cowboys no less. Jim and I even hit road games together—such as the AFC Championship on January 11, 1981. The Silver and Black Attack upset the favored 11–4 San Diego Chargers that day 34–27 becoming only the second wild card team ever to reach the Super Bowl.

The trip home proved even more memorable than the game. Returning to the Oakland Airport, the dark, evil side of Raider Nation awaited us. The scruffy motorcycle, Hells Angels types—who sat in the Black Hole behind the southern end zone—engaged in a heinous brawl with some rival gang. Greasy gang members whipped bike chains around, switchblades flashed, brass knuckles flew.

Initially, it didn't seem real, more like a movie, until you spotted people getting hurt. And I mean seriously hurt.

"C'mon, Jim. Let's get the hell outta here fast while we're still alive!" I grabbed his leathered arm and yanked.

"No way." Schock, my maniac friend, determined to put a stop to this all-out brawl instead dove right into the middle of the fray.

"Hey, we're all Ray-Duz fans here. What's goin' on? Put down those weapons," Schock pleaded. "We hafta get along with each other and win the Super Bowl."

They looked at him as if he were nuts—which of course, he was.

"Let's scram, Jim." I tugged harder on his sleeve, begging to no avail. "We're gonna get killed."

But damned if Schock didn't pull it off. He ran around releasing bikers from headlocks and other uncompromising positions, helped up bleeding victims. Eventually, he calmed everyone down. Next thing you knew, it was a Thug Hug Fest.

I finally pulled him away before everyone started singin' friggin' "Kumbaya" arm in arm for God's sake. Well, maybe not that bad, but the scene became mellow. At least I can say I saw one miracle in my life.

The Raiders ruled with Kenny the Snake, Stabler, Freddie Biletnikoff, Matt Millen out of Penn State, the Mad Stork, the Ghost to the Post, Gene Upshaw, Lester the Molester, and a guy partying all night in New Orleans before the Super Bowl who famously said, "If you wanna cruise with the Tooz, you're gonna bruise"—John Matuszak. What a colorful cast of characters—castoffs from other teams. What a load of fun that season had been. And the Raiders won Super Bowl XV versus Pennsylvania's Philadelphia Eagles.

But this all changed because of the arrival of the salt blanket.

CHAPTER 2

'81: THE SALT BLANKET

"HIYA, SWEETHEART. HOW are ya?" I tossed my bags into the corner of our sunny San Jose adobe. I kissed Joanne, noticing a lack of reciprocation in her perfunctory smooch. "Didja miss me?"

I had just returned from a week in the Rockies, hiking and camping with friends. "You're a little-pissed off, right? Leaving you home alone. But we talked about this before I left." Or so I thought.

She just stared or rather glared with a determined gaze. I checked out her hand. My engagement ring was missing. Shoot. Not good.

I'll cheer her up. "Joanne, look. I know I kept pushing our wedding back. I appreciate how this upsets you. We've been engaged a little longer than you've wanted."

"One and a half years. That is not a *little*." Icicles clung to each word.

I took her by both hands, noticing the smoothness. I stroked her long, also amazingly soft, honey-colored hair, remembering how much I *do* love this woman. "I stood on the top of Estes Park, atop the Rockies. Looking at the world below, I realized, I do love you."

An old familiar feeling was rising inside. "What good's seeing all that beauty and not sharing it? 'No more excuses,' I yelled over the canyon, hearing my echo confirm this. Let's plan the wedding today. I'm in."

"You mean no more 'Uncle Bunny can't make the wedding, so we must postpone'?" She leaned in, saying this in a wicked voice I never heard from her before.

"Exactly. I want to marry you." I swooped her up into my arms. "Whoever comes, comes, period. Forget the rest. Please, put the stone back on. Let's set the date in stone, okay?"

It worked. Fantastic. I smiled. My insides glowed. She shoved her pretty little head deep into my shoulder. I lifted her chin with my index finger. Her face looked sensitive, angelic, and—in love.

Look at those natural rosy cheeks. Everything about her was natural, all her beauty. I can't even describe how naturally well it felt hugging her. Thank God I knew how to read her perfectly. She was back. No longer hostile or distant. I was a fool putting this off. I wanted her forever. I loved her, needed her. She mumbled sweet words of love that I didn't quite hear.

I stepped back, holding her at arm's length. "What's that, my love? Sorry but I didn't quite catch that."

Oh look, I'd made her so happy her eyes rimmed with tears of joy. I bounced a quick kiss off her full pink lips, tasting the saltiness of her tears.

Looking me in the eye, her angelic voice rising, she repeated, "I said, I want to break up. It's over. I grew tired of waiting. I found someone else. I'm sorry."

A bright white solar blast ripped through my body. What? This can't be true. She fell back inside my arms then emptied her tears into my shoulder.

"Who? Who?"

"You don't know him, and it doesn't matter."

What the hell? Was she undoing my belt buckle? Now? Was she undressing me? I grabbed her wrists. If she thinks I'm going to make love to someone dumping me for another man, she's crazy. I do have some morals after all. That was the furthest thing from my mind.

However, this radiant energy needed to come out of me. It pressed against the inside of my skin, bursting outwards, air growing inside a balloon before exploding. Did she sense that?

"Let's make love one final time," she whispered in a silvery tone, unbearably sexy. "I'll still always love you." Her eyes stormy, hidden night lightning about to strike.

I shook my head no, stunned. "If you think I'm making love to a woman breaking my heart, you're sadly mistaken. I want no part of this. You insane?"

"Please?"

"Never."

I guess she figured now that she's told me, she could revert to her normal sweet self. I defiantly placed my hands firmly on my hips. She undressed. Her magnificent body, suddenly forbidden fruit, untouchable purity, no longer mine, there before me. Her tanned curvaceous body that would fill out any sweater.

I stared. "Uh . . . sorry, but there's no possible way," I repeated, noticing I mumbled as if my mouth were full of marbles. She could not possibly look any more beautiful than now, her usually perfectly parted-down-the-middle hair falling over her face perfectly. Her emerald-green eyes penetrating laser beam-like. I felt like a starving wolf in a meat shop.

She approached. Somehow, I found myself naked. Well, I only had on but three items—a T-shirt, shorts, and tighty-whities—to start with, so it didn't take much. It was like arriving on a hot summer day all sweaty because you had no AC in the car and diving into a country-fresh waterhole.

We embraced. I thought of getting her to the bedroom right down the hall. Too late for that. She pulled me down. We made passionate love right on the hardwood, she crying her bloody eyes out hysterically, saying, "I'm so sorry" the whole time. Her salty tears covered us like a blanket

It felt great. It felt dreadful. A real mystery.

CHAPTER 3

LIFE'S THREE BIGGEST MYSTERIES

"LET ME TELL you, brother. Making love to a woman for the final time—crying hysterically throughout—well, it's . . . it's impossible to describe."

"That's some heavy shit, man," Van replied, pulling his long hair through a rubber band and into a ponytail. "Quite the story. Can't say I ever made love to a crying woman. But if I had to make love to you, believe me, I'd be crying too."

No one was more sarcastic than Van.

"Thanks. You're so damn sympathetic. It's only been a month for God's sake. Check this out: we met August 4, 1977, and broke up August 4, 1981—four years to the day. Weird, right?"

"That means it was meant to be. Dude, lissen'"—he caught my eye—"you gotta move on. You're doing the right things. You leased out the house after she moved her shit out. You scored a nice pad right here in the Cow Hollow for Chrissakes." He looked around. "Right in the Marina District near the bay. Place is crawling with chicks. You can't mope around the rest of your life with this broken-heart syndrome bullshit."

Guy had insight. "But that's exactly how it feels. Like my actual heart physically broke. It's sore. It hurts. I finally know what heartbreak truly means."

The stone-fox waitress arrived with our breakfast and the second round of double Bloody Marys.

Van grabbed then slugged his, saying, "This is usually all I need for breakfast."

I'll listen to Van's advice. The dude does know about stuff. Strangers he's never met call him when they visit the Bay Area, asking what shows to see, what's happening. He should write an advice column really.

"There are plenty of birds in the ocean." He launched an assault on his eggs Benedict that would make a Viking proud.

"What? Wait. Never mind. You don't understand, Van. I only love her. I'm going to do whatever it takes to win her back. We lived together my entire final term at Penn State when I moved her into my frat room. We drove 3,000 miles to get out here to California together. Started a new life together. Bought our first house together. Four full years living together. Walked the midnight beaches of Hawaii together."

"Yeah, I know all that, and now you broke up together. Deal with it."

"What about those promises she and I made on that beach in Hawaii, lying on our backs under all those stars, holding hands? Hell, I don't even get a warning?"

"Don't be an idiot, fool. She probably gave you tons of warnings. You didn't see them was all. Try to remember—you're not a very bright guy. She didn't want to just live together anymore like you did. She wanted a traditional marriage, to have kids, settle down, all that shit. Deep inside, you didn't obviously. You made the choice, not her. You kept passing the buck and wanting to get the milk for free without buying the cow as the motherhood says. So shut the hell up and live with your choice. Like we agreed, just keep super busy. Let some water pass under the bridge. Now, pass the Tabasco."

I furrowed my brows. My ears burned as if that was where I applied the Tabasco. I hated the truth. Hated it.

"Yes, keep super busy at all cost, avoid inner feelings. Monday through Friday? No sweat—I worked like a banshee downtown until it was late, work out half to death at the gym, then pass out exhausted at night. Saturdays, I party with you guys. But Sundays in San Francisco? Either everyone's with their families and mine's back east, or everyone's doing brunch with their lovers. It's a day for couples, dude. Gotta find something to do Sundays, get my mind off things."

Just then a couple walked by holding hands, down Van Ness Avenue, past the massive window in front of our seats in the City

Tavern, heading toward Chrissy Field to sunbathe, grill, or play beach volleyball. I couldn't stand it. I wanted what they got. What I had but royally blew it.

Van broke the city silence. "Don't you love skiing? Be a ski bum and burn that butt-ugly three-piece suit of yours."

I looked first at my Brooks Brothers custom-made wool three-piece then at Van in his hooded tie-dyed hippie shirt made from pure hemp. Cutoff shorts he designed himself with a buck knife. A hippie pouch tethered to his belt accented with the gigantic buckle. I could only imagine what onlookers thought of us. We made quite the pair. I worked with other suits all week deep in the bowels of San Francisco's Financial District, lost in the corporate world. Van, hair flowing beyond his waist, enjoyed getting wasted, and wasting time was fine. He knew no stress. Unlike me. I go ballistic whenever I'm wasting time.

Gotta stay busy. Keep my mind off despair and her cousin gloom. I felt hollow inside, abandoned, and powerless.

I said, "Absolutely, man. I dig skiing. I envy the hell outta ski instructors. They thumb their noses at Corporate America while they skied nonstop."

"So there ya go." He drank heartily from his Bloody Mary, wiping the wet red away from his mouth with the back of his hand. He's an earthy one this one.

"But it's a four-hour commute to Lake Tahoe," I added. "Too much. And with autumn just beginning, September and October are the warmest months of the year. No one's skiing for many moons."

"Well, warm days what's cool living out here compared to the east. How 'bout working in wine tasting? Napa or Sonoma Valley wineries? Sundays are huge up there."

"True, they're nearby too."

Hmm, was that a possibility? I picked up and tilted my Bloody Mary, examining it inside the sunbeam shooting into our restaurant. I poured some into Van's empty water glass. "This wine we're pouring today, sir, is complex yet unassuming, with just a hint of a velvety almond on the back end. Please note the tannic finish."

Van shook his head in disgust. "Really?"

"Nah, plus since God gave me zero willpower, I'd end up drinking wine before it's time."

"How 'bout a book reading club? You always got your face shoved in a book like some geek."

"Bor-ing. I gotta come up with something. Yesterday, I went out of my mind. I was suicidal."

"Weekend traveling?"

"I travel way too much for work the way it is. Look, I wanna enjoy my time living in the heart of the City. Pass the salt."

He passed both salt and pepper. "So think, asshole. What's one thing you love?"

"Football."

We both laughed. "Wouldn't it be great if I worked *that* in somehow? Last year, catching every home game of the Raiders with Schock and Tom Resor all the way to the Super Bowl, man, that was epic."

He said, "Yeah, but now you've moved into the beating heart of Niner country."

Suddenly, his pager started hopping around the table like a frog on a hot coal stove. He ran outside, slid into the phone booth, and grabbed a pay phone I wouldn't touch with a pair of tongs.

I sipped on my just-arrived cup of premium coffee, noticing the smoothness and clean Colombian aftertaste. Sinatra crooned in the background—of course about his broken heart. I went back to my problem: what to do on Sundays? Look, how much time I spent thinking about football now that the season's almost here? *Was* there a football angle? I know it sounded ridiculous, but hey, wait a sec. What if I . . .

Just as I had formulated that complete thought, Van crashed it, slamming back down into his seat. Darn. His work done, he resumed his attack on *my* remaining eggs Benedict. But I had something there, something like—

Now our waitress crashed the train of thought by bringing the bill Van snatched, saying, "I got this one" and flashed his one-minute-old wad of cash.

I clutched my heart and crashed to the floor. "Good God. This is the big one."

"Get up, asshole," he said. "I pay all the time. More'n you do."

"I don't think so." I crawled back into my seat and dusted my suit off, digging the smirk on his ugly mug, my thought unconsciously returned.

"Got it. Hey, Van. I just had an epiphany!"

"A what?"

"Never mind. I forgot your vocabulary maxes out at two syllables. You remember that Niners game?"

"Yeah. They sucked. Cowboys blew'em out 59–13. The Cowboys were pointing at them and laughing. The 49ers are unwatchable. What about it?"

"Remember me mentioning how close to the action the security guards stood?"

"Actually, no." He gave me his patented smile, teeth like white Chicklet gum.

"That's 'cos that shit your smoking's doing a number on your memory. Anyway, I just now thought about those guys. I mean, they're right on the freaking field of play. They stand around, watching the crowd. How hard would it be to turn your head and watch the action? First time I'd ever thought about those invisible yet very visible guys *everywhere* once you noticed 'em. A paradox, right?"

"I know nuthin' about 'em."

"Figures. My God. Look at the time. Gotta run. Thanks for breakfast." We shook thumbs, which unfortunately was still in style.

"So, I'll score *three* tickets for the Tull Show?" Van yelled as I was leaving.

Van always had a steady girlfriend—unlike me. Three meant I was a loser who couldn't even scrape up my end for a double date.

"Yes. I just love being the third wheel."

I flew outside, hoofed it uphill on Van Ness Avenue, and hopped onto America's only moving national monument, the cable car. I headed downtown on the California Line into the Financial District. But now at least I had hope, hope to escape scary Sunday syndrome.

I hustled into Friday's Financial District routine: work until 5:30 PM, hit Lilly's in the Embarcadero for happy hours, dance to a fifties retro band called the Cadillacs, dine on Union Street with a group at a restaurant called Perry's.

There, I consumed the soft Dungeness crab, the freshly baked sourdough bread, and washed it all down with the local brew, Anchor Steam, then, as usual, got lost in the Bermuda Triangle—three bars on three corners in the Marina District. This routine rocked. No plans needed. Stay in your canoe and follow the current. You get to know everyone with this same weekly habit. I may not have been able to find anyone to replace Joanne, but at least I *could* do some serious networking, find out what was happening—and I did.

Around midnight, I called Van. "Hey, bro, guess what I found out? An organization called Burns Security owns the contract providing the Forty-Niners with security. I'm gonna call them tomorrow and interview for a part-time security guard."

Van replied, "Don't be stupid. You don't think those positions would be long gone by now. Preseason's ready to start. You'll just be wasting your time."

"Thanks for the encouragement, *friend*."

I called first thing Monday anyway, and surprisingly, they immediately set up an interview. No other details were given other than the boss agreed to see me in his office in the China Basin.

Tuesday morning, possessing absolutely no security experience whatsoever, I hoofed it over for the interview. However, on the way there, I thought about how the field jobs *had* to be taken like Van so gracefully mentioned.

There will most likely be a waiting list. Maybe in a few years, my name will pop up. Probably have to know someone to get in. That's always the case. I know nobody. I thought of pulling a U-turn but instead trudged on. As I always said, what's the worst that can happen if it involved no physical pain? Besides, I had to fill those Sundays with something, or this rotten heartbreak, I'm telling you, it was unbearable. Made me feel worthless. Had to try.

The interview lasted a whopping twenty minutes, half of which was filling out the application. Walking back in a reflective mood, I thought, you know, the three biggest mysteries I had ever known were

(1) Stonehenge: no one knows how or why those stones got there all the way from Wales circa 2600 B.C. (2) Easter Island: when Captain Cook arrived on Thursday, March 17, 1774, and found those amazing Moai statues, he asked to meet the oldest inhabitant on the island to find out the history. The elder chief told him that he *also* asked *his* elderly grandparents that same damn question, and they too were clueless (3) The 49er security job: turns out they *des*perately needed security guards. The local San Franciscans did not gobble those jobs up like someone named Van told me. Burns Security—assuming my background checked out—hired me on the spot.

I remembered that Woody Allen quote: "Success was 85 percent just showing up." I smiled for the first time all month.

The smiling did not last long, however. Covering both myself and the entire city of San Francisco were the ensuing dark shadows.

CHAPTER 4

'81: DARK SHADOWS

MY NEW PART-TIME career began in earnest. My first preseason game was ensconced so deep within the famous low San Francisco fog, I didn't even know which way to face. You couldn't see your hand held in front of your eyes. The steady drizzling rain surely but steadily soaked everything, from the drizzling rain inside the cloud to full-on rain. We were literally under sea level on days like this, Candlestick Park being right on the Bay. I skipped the mandatory meeting on "Careers within the Security Industry" and sloshed toward the field to catch a little action, maybe break the dismal mood.

My dark times paralleled San Francisco's perfectly. The entire city was ensconced in mourning. Former supervisor Dan White brutally assassinated the City's beloved Mayor, George Moscone, on November 27, 1978. White also murdered the voice of the gay movement, Harvey Milk. The new mayor, Dianne Feinstein, struggled trying to pull all the fragments back together down in City Hall.

On top of all this, just one week earlier, the Jonestown mass suicide in Guyana, originating out of San Francisco, shook the city like an earthquake. San Francisco was where the evil Reverend James Jones's headquarters controlled a cult of over 20,000 members. The 909 people, many from the City, drank the Kool-Aid and died of cyanide poisoning.

On July 15, President Jimmy Carter gave his infamous malaise speech and said, "America is threatened by a crisis in confidence." He then promptly fired his cabinet, putting the country into chaos.

On November 4, 1979, the Iran hostage crisis began the embarrassing 444 days of captivity. Reading the daily count in the headlines each morning was like starting your day with another papercut between your toes. Interest rates, as high as 17 percent for a basic first deed of trust, crippled the economy. Gas prices soared because of the full-blown energy crisis and OPEC. Americans seethed in long gas lines.

These stories dominating the news cast dark shadows over San Francisco's golden hue. I remember thinking, *This ain't the Summer of Love.*

The coaches pulled the starters from the game early because the game, like my life, meant nothing. Zilch. Nothing mattered. I had taken to mindlessly walking while staring down at my feet. The mud from the field's sidelines climbed over the line of my shoes and entered like a rat crawling into its nest.

The rain backed the sewer system up, thus adding to the ambience. The fans bailed out long ago, and the empty stadium looked eerie. Everything felt dark, dank, drab, and diabolically miserable. In short, it was perfect for my mood. The Niners, as usual, lost to the Chargers. No one cared.

The next home preseason game El Capitán, who must've known I was a jag-off by now, took me into what they called the War Room. A full uniform—white shirt, blue tie, blue pants with a stripe down the side, and shiny black shoes—wrapped around his skinny, skeletal frame, and he casually slid around the room like a cat creeping through high grass.

"You work in a regular office, right? How 'bout organizing this room?" He pulled out a drawer stuffed with files. "Put things in order. This economy means I have huge budget cuts to deal with, less full-time guards, fewer salaries, fewer benefits paid. So, more part-timers like you guys. You, part-timers, can meet here during the season before each game. Go over these field books, manuals, guidelines, plan your strategies, and here, look at all the files we have." He opened and closed a few drawers, stacked like concrete. "See what you can do."

I just shook my head. I was too busy feeling sorry for myself to take on any projects. I never thought Joanne would leave me for another. Immediately, I ordered up dozens of Hefty bags then tossed nearly all the black binders filled with nonsense into them. Next, I yanked out handfuls of random files from their drawers and glanced them over. "Candlestick

Communications Systems," « In Case of Emergency," « Security Guard Handbooks," some looked like instruction manuals from World War I.

Dumping every other file into the Hefties, I had them hauled off to the gigantic green dumpster seemingly attached to the concrete wall of Candlestick Park at the bottom of the ramp, right outside the gate. Who cared about anything anymore anyway?

Two weeks later, before the Oakland Raiders Battle of the Bay game, El Capitán slipped into the War Room where I sat with other guards. He *did* have that official look.

He looked around and said, "My, you've done wonders to this room. Guess you put a lot of stuff in our storage lockers below, right?"

I stood, clicked my heels, and saluted. "Everything is where it needs to be, El Capitán, sir."

"Well, good job. This room looks organized." He left with two full-timers shadowing him as always.

I said, "Thanks" and went back to my deep brooding until an unexpected, fascinating phenomenon occurred.

CHAPTER 5

F-BOMBS

BUT THEN ONE day *poof*! Inexplicably, the entire scene enveloping me changed dramatically. The regular season began. I took notice of the phenomenon: the entire Bay Area went absolutely zonkers over their San Francisco 49ers. Same on the East Bay side with the Oakland Raiders. Whenever there are discussions about the craziest football cities, both San Francisco and Oakland *must* be in those discussions. Living on the Peninsula, you couldn't help keeping up with the 49ers. The front pages of the *San Francisco Chronicle* and *San Jose Mercury News* each day, the daily features in the Green Pages (the sports section), nonstop radio chatter, and even billboards shouted every trade, every move, every quote by the owner, coach, or various players.

I remember catching this when living in the South Bay (San Jose) all those years. How at work, the Monday morning discussions inside the boardrooms centered on how god-awful the Forty-Niners were again this year. How they creatively found ways to blow the game. Friends like Bob Halstead, who bled burgundy and gold since he was a baby, came into our Monday morning meetings, saying, "Those Forty-Fuckin'-Niners once again snatched a loss from the jaws of victory."

F-bombs exploded all over the office from executive management to the clerical staff. Men, women, children, old, young, white, Hispanic, Asian, black, short or tall, it didn't matter—everyone cursed. Everyone was dialed in. Everyone was *not pleased*. And that was San Jose!

Now living in the heart of the City, I saw the Niners were a part of the very fabric of San Francisco. And this was a terrible team, one of the worst in history. Imagine what this place would be like if they ever had even a decent team?

The Forty-Fuckin'-Niners lost their opening game on the road to perennial doormats Detroit, the Niners shooting themselves in the foot in the closing minutes.

Bob, solid buddy, work partner, also my next-door neighbor, lived in an apartment above Joanne and me before we bought our house. Bob, tall, the son of WASPs, sported light blond hair, wore round glasses, and was rather shy until you got to know him. He sympathized with me about my terrible heartache. We did lunch, whipped out our brown paper bags, and launched into a serious discussion about the upcoming season.

"Tell me, Rick. How is it being a security guard for such a rotten team?"

"Well, I've only worked exhibition games thus far. No one takes 'em seriously. I just wander around aimlessly. Only real work I did was clean out a meeting room. That took five minutes. I'll find out what my role will be when we get our assignments this Sunday, our first home game—against Walter Payton and the Bears."

"I pray it's not another tortuous season. In '78, the Forty-Fuckin-Niners ranked dead last in total offense. That's offensive. In '79, they won two whole games after starting the season 0–7. They finished 2–14. They've had losing records seven out of the last eight years. It's all rather embarrassing."

"Well, last year they went, what? 6–10? Losing record, I know, but hey, that's still an improvement, right?" I chomped into my tuna-fish sandwich. "Whad'ya think of their new coach?" I asked in a muffled voice.

"Bill Walsh?" Bob rubbed the nape of his neck. "I dunno. The pundits are already calling for his head. Eddie DeBartolo, the new owner, was ambitious. He pulled the forty-seven-year-old Walsh right off Stanford's campus. Coach Walsh has zero pro-head-coaching experience. College coaches never make it in the pros. Name one. Go 'head. Guy won two whole games in '79. But supposedly, he's the cerebral type and has a new approach to coaching. We'll see. We talked like this over the last GM Eddie D hired, Joe Thomas, a loser."

"Well, I do kinda like how he's been drafting. Four of his first five picks were defensive backs. Crazy, right? I heard he's also focused on, as John Madden would say, 'the Big Uglies: the linemen who make or break your team.'"

"And he scored a solid wide receiver in Dwight Clark with a tenth-round pick. Dwight's looked amazing so far, a future superstar." I offered Bob some of my Lay's potato chips.

Bob, clearly irritated as only a lifelong Niner fan of perhaps the worst franchise in all of sports could be, waved my bag away. "Bill Walsh also is under fire for his other draft choices. The press feels Walsh wasted a third-round pick on that skinny kid from Notre Dame. He passed on other available quarterbacks. Now the final pick of the third round is the starter? This QB was the eighty-second guy taken. I don't mind him so much. My dad and other hard cores wanted the Niners to go with their experienced quarterback, Steve DeBerg. Not some average Joe—a Joe Montana." Bob clenched his teeth and shoved the remainder of his lunch away.

I'd better change the subject, like, back to me. "Anyways, I even get paid to do this. Seven bucks an hour. But I'd've worked for free. Keeps me busy all day Sunday."

"Sounds good. What's the worst part?"

"Being forced to wear a *short* sleeve white shirt, 100 percent polyester."

Bob and I shared a laugh. Good. Got him out of the doldrums.

I continued, "Being obsessed with clothing and a bona fide disciple of *Dress for Success* by John Mallory"—I extended my hands downward in a manner showing my custom-fitted three-piece Italian wool suit— "The polyester security uniform I'm forced to wear is disturbing, an obvious assault on good taste and decency. Compounding the problem further, the brass, who runs this operation like the military, makes you wear the company-sanctioned, you ready for this?"

Bob nodded, clearly amused.

"Blue *clip-on ties* each Sunday. Ouch. Help me. Another attack on good fashion and taste. The bottom of my tie doesn't even reach the friggin' belt buckle. A faux pas if there ever was one. Whenever my blue blazer opens, everyone could easily spot a tie extending only halfway down my shirt, stopping above my belly button—highlighted by the polyester whiteness behind it. Egads!"

Bob laughed heartily. "You're bumming. Plus, the seventies are over, dude," he added. "When football was strictly a male bastion. There are tons of foxy ladies attending these games nowadays checking out your polyester look."

"You don't have to tell me. Yeah, the Niners suck, but even in preseason, they still sell out, and you're right—half the crowd's chicks these days. But it's okay. I'm not wearing that crap any longer."

"Why? What're you gonna do about it?" Bob looked at his watch and stood.

"Well," I also stood, rolled the bag into a ball, and missed my shot into the green wastebasket. "We open the season at Candlestick this Sunday . . . and I've got a plan."

That Friday, I visited the clothier on Montgomery Street, Brooks Brothers, in the Financial District. I brought in my military garb to match. I loved the tailors working in there, how they spoke, moved.

I showed up for my first regular-season Sunday game wearing a custom-fit white 100 percent light-cotton shirt and a Pucci Italian silk tie. No one would notice. It matched perfectly.

Inside Candlestick, I punched in wearing my blue Burns Security Blazer all buttoned up and waved to El Capitán behind his desk burning an unfiltered Kool. He gave me his usual grunt. He was going with the white stubble look all over his face for opening day. Guy doesn't even know I'm alive. My new clothing scheme worked perfectly. No one detected a thing. Ha. Beautiful. I felt *so* much better wearing finer threads and not that despicable polyester that doesn't even breathe. "Clothes make the man," Mark Twain said. "Naked people have little or no influence on society," he also added.

I sauntered outside and found the well-fed lieutenant to obtain my season's assignment. During the preseason, I often followed this chubby guy nicknamed Father Goose around ad nauseam as he chattered nonstop into his walkie-talkie. This guy was *way* too into his job. He never as so much as glanced toward the action on the field. A group of us followed him as he dropped each of us little ducklings off at our assignment. Only I remained, surprised as he led me back to the main office, all the while babbling into his beloved black box.

"Boss wants you," he said, always expressionless, opening the door.

Sitting behind his desk, I noted El Capitán's leathery face. It looked like a walnut. First time I'd seen him with his cap off. Black hair combed straight back. I thought, man, he was skinny. Kind of guy that when he got hungry, he fired up a smoke instead.

Just as during our interview, he used words like a sniper used bullets—sparingly.

"Take that off. Put *your* uniform on. Shake your ass. The lieutenant's waiting."

Shit. How'd he know? I slipped back into the irritating white 100 percent polyester shirt, frowned while topping it off with my polyester clip-on tie, pulled up the polyester pants, so stiff I swear they could stand on their own. You could shave with the permanent razorlike crease in them. I topped the entire ensemble off with a bright fire-red truck cap stamped *Security*.

El Capitán handed me my same blue blazer. "Don't do that again. Here's your badge. Lieutenant, take him to his assigned area. Go."

I pinned the shiny gold badge onto my jacket. Ahhh . . . at least there was one piece of uniform I dug. Like your first car or your first girl, you never forget your first badge.

Another gaggle of geese awaited me, and once again, we followed the waddling main goose.

"What on earth could Father Goose constantly be yakking about in that damn walkie-talkie? There's hardly any fans here yet," I asked a fellow guard as we waited on an upper deck while Father Goose gave instructions for manning this particular area.

"No idea. By the way, my name is Gunner."

Gunner looked and acted clever. He was short, sharp, mischievous with pointed teeth. His eyes, resembling ball bearings, kept shooting around. He said, "This is my pal, Brad, we joined together last season."

Brad, extremely tall, too tall for his own skin and not quite as sharp as Gunner. He had a permanent Pepsodent grin. Brad had perfectly red eyes. Under his cap sat a head of hair his cap could only lie upon. But he seemed nice. Gunner's cap was the opposite—pulled down as far as possible, just above his sharp, darting eyes. Together, they reminded me of George and Lennie from Steinbeck's *Of Mice and Men*.

"He sooo fuckin' serious about bein' a guard." Gunner shot me the look. "Not like you and us. We're here strictly to be up close to the action, aren't we, Rick?"

That sarcastic remark surprised me because it was true. "Holy cow. Am I that obvious?"

Tall Brad, with his baby face and resembling an Ivy Leaguer, looked down upon me and grinned. "This is our second year. We see which guards are in it for the job. We caught you watching the games. You couldn't resist, even meaningless preseason games. You're like us. But don't worry. We'll keep it on the down-low." Then Brad looked at his oversized Mickey Mouse watch and announced the time as I later learned, was his habit.

Gunner offered me, of all things, a toothpick. "They're flavored." I chose the mint over the cinnamon. He continued, "Forty-Niner games always sell out. The huge waiting list for season tickets is legendary. On game day, scalpers charge a small ransom to get into the Stick—to see a *losing* team. Can you imagine if the Niners ever had a damn *winning* team? So we do this. We're not here for some second career, right?"

"Yeah, right," I lied. He need not know I'm doing this to keep my mind off of Joanne. By the way, what if she doesn't come back? That's how it's looking. I know I can never ever, ever replace her. I'll have to wander the earth, alone forever.

I held back another panic attack, pondering this lifetime sentence of hell. Fortunately, the procession continued down the concrete ramp. Once again, we resembled ducklings waddling after Father Goose, the too-into-it lieutenant in charge. He continued positioning us, brand-new part-time security guards, into the spots for our season-long assignments. The fans began filling the stadium.

My two new friends peeled off. I was last. Father Goose was going to give me a shit assignment. First, there was the fashion faux pas I tried slipping past El Capitán. I duplicated my polyester uniform ensemble with cotton look-alikes perfectly, yet he busted me. Secondly, since Gunner and Brad knew, I'll bet El Capitán knew too. Damn, he's on to me.

I looked out into the deep, vast regions beyond the goal posts, miles from the action. Some guard, from this angle, looked two inches tall as he waved to us. Fans actually sat way back there? Why?

Father Goose ushered me toward that spot deep into Siberia's frozen tundra. I'll be in charge of herding yaks and opening trade routes for the Mongolians while the icy winds whipped the winter land.

He took a shortcut and walked onto the field. I thought that was a no-no. However, it was way cool down here. Suddenly, the Goose honked, "Here's your spot."

Slack-jawed, I watched him waddle off, blathering into his black box, then I let out a blood-curdling scream.

CHAPTER 6

THUNDER ON THE FIELD

ON MY LEFT side as I faced the field, a giant of a man stared down at me. Blood of my blood! It just happened to be R. C. Owens.

Huge, black as molasses, he extended gargantuan hands wrapped around bright white palms. What's he doing? He suddenly dropped about twenty pounds of hand upon my shoulders. He fixed his large, yellowish watery eyes on me. He donned a gold sports coat and a pomp of age-whitened African hair. His bright white smile relaxed me a bit. Still, I continued staring into the milky eyes of the inventor of the famous alley-oop catch from his heydays as a 49er.

Quarterback Y. A. Tittle would throw it up there and R. C., using his height and remarkable jumping ability, went up to catch it. The alley-Oop pass lives in our current vernacular, especially in the NBA, to this very day. Dude even stood under the goal post and blocked a field goal once.[1]

"Watchu screamin for?" he thundered from above, shaking his head from side to side, wearing a bright gold Forty-Niners sports jacket.

I looked up at the gentle giant and answered. "That's 'cos I pinched myself hard so I'd wake up from this dream."

We gazed out over the too-good-to-be-true bright green field with the fifty-yard line cutting across. Looking up, I saw the sea of orange-gold seating. I dizzily leaned my right hand on the grainy Forty-Niner bench. This was the best spot to view a game in the entire ballpark.

---

1   The following year, because of him, the NFL outlawed that goaltending play. Owens's best year was 1961, when he gained over 1,000 yards receiving.

"Ha. And this is who'll be guarding us this season? A screamer? We're screwed."

I hadn't even noticed that I stood between *two* men, R. C and one other to my right. I spun around and shook the hand of a then-famous standup comedian Bob Sarlatte. Bob who performed regularly on *Late Night with David Letterman* show was a wildly popular radio and TV personality throughout the Bay Area and across the nation. We pumped hands furiously.

"Tell us one. Go 'head, Bob," crackled R. C from somewhere above.

Bob: "I went to a baseball game up in Toronto. The crowd was small."

R. C. and I: "How small was it?"

Bob: "The crowd was *so* small, the vendors waited for you while you finished eating before yelling, '*Hot dog*! Who needs a hot dog?'"

Okay, maybe you had to be there.

Bob was a comedian for a reason. He'd constantly crack up R. C. and me with classic one-liners throughout every game. Watching R. C. slapping his thighs, busting up, and falling apart from Bob's in-the-moment jokes was funnier than the lines themselves.

Best of all, Bob had a sweet table with my name on it right down front whenever he performed at the Punchline or Cobbs Comedy Club in the City. Not a bad option to drag a date for lonely single guys like me. Not that those dates ever led to anything, but why go there?

Wait a sec. What was a standup comic doing at the bench?

As I pondered this, *Holy sh*t! Earthquake! Is this the real deal?*

Above and around us, the entire stadium suddenly shook. I mean it rocked. I never experienced this before. Jerking my head upward, I saw that the wild view from the field was overwhelming. Everything was so high above us. Place was packed to the gills. You couldn't get another fan in here with a shoehorn. The stadium continued shaking as the fans began slamming their feet up and down. You could see the seating visibly move, earthquake style. The stadium came alive, almost literally.

Then I heard Bob's radio voice bellowing in my head. *What the—?*

Twirling around I noted Bob had grabbed a microphone from the small stand and proceeded to announce the pregame starting lineups.

The players sprinted onto the field, but only after hearing that distinct Bob Sarlatte voice. The voice of the Forty-Niners stood right next to me. I could have grabbed the mike and yelled anything, like, "Let's go, Raiders" to the sold-out, now-standing audience. I didn't but Bob said plenty. He would continue as the voice of the Forty-Niners for thirty seasons.

Bob slowly announced, "From Notre Dame, number 16, Joe . . . Montana."

Joe jogged onto the field under a perpetual roar from the crowd, cheers and a few boos, mainly from the DeBerg fans still loyal to the veteran QB, but mostly cheers.

Then the remainder of the team thundered across the field as if the Roman legions in gold helmets and deep red tunics were attacking. I was thunderstruck. The earth jumped from the pounding of the cleats.

Suddenly, I was smack-dab in the middle of the colorful forty-nine-member team roster as players scurried all around me. Was I supposed to be here? Massive goliaths pounding each other's shoulder pads while screaming psyched-up words full blast. Coaches were in player's faces barking out last-minute instructions. A cacophony of sounds flew into the adrenaline-soaked Candlestick air.

You could smell the freshly laundered uniforms; the Ajax smelling salts players cracked open, pressed into their nostrils, inhaling the ammonia deeply and screaming upward to their gods as that unique metallic, rusty locker-room smell lingered.

As the players loosened up, I heard deafening crowd cheers led by the 49er cheerleaders. This *certainly* was no preseason game. The intensity caught me by surprise. This was the start of the season, a new decade, the beginning of Eddie DeBartolo's new family-ownership style and what would become a new-look 49ers era.

Montana warmed up behind the bench firing missiles to Dwight Clark who stood next to me while I faced the crowd. Dwight, number 87, would softly toss it back to whomever the second-string quarterback was at the time who, in turn, would launch it to Joe's ball catcher.

RICK PUCCI

Yes, a professional ball catcher. QBs can't risk getting their pinkies dinged by catching warmup balls. Joe fired another, whistling through the air before it smacked into Clark's formidable hands. I stepped in and picked one off. Then I flipped it back to Dwight to toss back to Joe's ball catcher. I smiled. They got a kick out of that, right? Now I could always ask my grandchildren, "Did I ever tell you about the time I intercepted a Joe Montana pass?"

Well, in my imagination I did anyway. I chickened out. I was a rookie too. Joe had been a part-time rookie himself last year and was still an experiment. This would be his first true season under center. He was not particularly famous at the time and surely had not yet become *the* Joe Montana. He wouldn't even be around much longer if he wasn't up to the challenge.

Later, Bob announced his usual mundane halftime activities in his pitch-perfect voice. But first, he checked his mic and then, out of the side of his mouth, made a private crack to R. C. and me as a local high school band marched on to the field: "Ladies and gentlemen, please give it up for the Immature Marching Band from Bumfuck Egypt."

We howled, of course, while he turned on his mic and professionalism to announce the real name into the echoing Candlestick PA system. That guy was too funny.

Lost on the sidelines in the midst of NFL icons, I wasn't quite invisible, but as a Burns Security guard, I was just window dressing. People *thought* security was all around when they glimpsed *Security* scrawled across our backs. That put their minds at ease—we weren't part of the show, but they knew we were there.

The coin toss. My heart pumped as I casually strolled alongside the bench that I assumed I was guarding. From what was always a mystery, would some deranged fan, pissed off over the Niners losing yet another one, grab a hammer and charge the field, attacking 300-pound-plus linemen? If I spotted something weird up in the bleachers, what would I do, and who would I even tell? I must have missed an instruction video somewhere.

My biggest fear: Father Goose waddles down here and asks, "What the hell are you doing in the middle of the team fer Chrissakes? I told you to do *this* instead."

But looking around, he was nowhere in sight.

I was a few angles short of a square but started to grow more adventurous, so I continued my stroll along the bench, trailing my finger on the wooden back where the Niners sat, and feeling a little bit cocky, I spotted Pete Kugler sitting right in the middle. Here was a lineman I recognized. Coach Walsh drafted Pete, a fellow native Pennsylvanian from my alma mater, Penn State. Pete would play ten NFL seasons as a premier nose tackle run stopper, an All-Pro who would garner three Super Bowl rings with the Niners. I smacked his shoulder pad and gave the traditional, "We *are*."

Pete looked up and instinctively said, "Penn State." We bonded.

Randy Cross, number 51, a guard on the team sitting next to Pete, glanced at me with a wry smile tucked under his thick black mustache. Randy may have been on to me. I pushed this far enough, so I gingerly slipped back to my spot and worried. Had I crossed the line?

No one ever told me what the line nor what my job was. The other guards around the field, stationed thirty yards apart, stared up at the crowd, so I did too.

Here I was, so long as I didn't blow it, a derelict from a backwater town in the Poconos Mountains, holding my spot between R. C. Owens and Bob Sarlatte, glaring into the crowd, a mere few feet away from Bill Walsh talking to Joe Montana. I could hear them. They're going over the first few plays they will run. Is this a great country or what?

The 49ers won the toss. Coach Walsh knelt directly behind me, giving Joe, who also knelt, some last-minute instructions. I could have heard them better had the crowd not been so damn loud. The two kept going over the set list. Turns out Coach, I later learned, choreographed the first series of offensive plays. Ingenious.

Game time.

The crowd was way louder down on the field. You don't just hear the roar on the sidelines—you feel it in your soul. It rumbled. I not only caught every play, but I also soaked up everything else on the bench, the part the fans don't see or hear—even those in the stadium. Fascinating. I knew I had to capture these initial memories in writing, so I began thinking of notes I could make as soon as I could get to pen and paper. I had to get this initial memory down in writing so I would never forget it.

At halftime, I sprinted to my locker, yanked my Daytimers book from my backpack and scribbled down my top three impressions. One never forgets first impressions:

The very first thing I noticed *immediately*: how impossibly *quick* NFL players were. Not just fast but their quickness, the ability to shift, turn, stop and pop with speed and grace. The game slows down from the distance of the stands and the television screen—I had never really *seen* the game before until I saw and felt it from the field level. Watching the Raider games last season from the stands could not compare. These guys had *animal* quickness and reflexes. Shocking. And the intense collisions, *hearing* them as well as seeing them. Two trucks smashing into each other head-on. *Mamma Mia, it was intense.*

You don't catch this on television nor from even from fifty-yard-line seats, only down here on the field. I never knew this. Plus, I wondered how many light-years away the teams I played on must have been.

Now I can appreciate that article I read by Marc Safran. As director of sports medicine at UCSF, Marc was also down here on the Niners sidelines helping with the nonstop injuries. He wrote,

> Television does not begin to convey the extraordinary size of pro football players, the freakish speed at which they move and the bone-rattling brutality of their collisions. When you're on the sidelines, and these guys go past you, it's almost like a herd of horses . . . You feel like the ground really shakes."[2]

My second first impression: learning how photographers obtain those great action shots. How do they do that? Their work seems magical. I always imagined the ace photographer angling his camera then timing that click at just the right time. However, it's not even remotely like that. The play begins. Photographers lined the entire field on black kneepads, taking photos in rapid succession, nonstop, flying through a roll of film on a single play. The sound of zipping cameras *click-click-clicking* away *was* the official sound of the game. It might be different today with digital equipment, but in the '80s the clicking cameras were alive on the sidelines. The photographers simply sent all those images to *Sports Illustrated,* the *AP*, or wherever. Someone there sifts through the hundreds of photos in hopes of catching that *one* glamour shot that will make the papers and magazines. When the

---

2   www.sfgate.com/sports/kroichick/article/Glory-has-its-price-25-years-later-the-heroes-2655062.php January 21, 2007, twenty-five years later, the heroes of the 49ers' first Super Bowl championship weigh the costs of playing a brutal game, by Ron Kroichick, *San Francisco Chronicle* staff writer

game ends, thousands of empty black plastic film canisters littered the surrounding sidelines.

I befriended a professional photographer who set up on the forty-yard line each game. We had a friendly quid pro quo relationship. I would escort him into security-only locations. He allowed me the ability to take killer action shots using his professional camera, like this action shot of Joe under center, Randy Cross to his right:

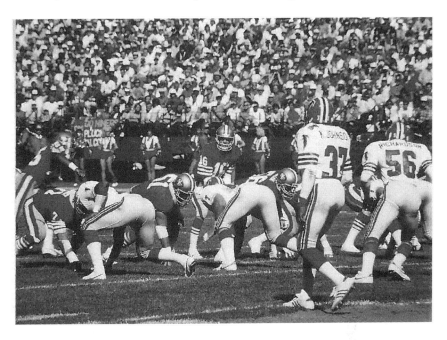

Number 3, since my actual job was monitoring the Niner crowd each Sunday, rather than just absorbing the games themselves, I noticed much about them from my unique vantage point. I especially adored how this audience was more akin to a collegiate crowd with *traditional* cheers than a professional football crowd. That's uniquely Niner. Then couple that with constant interaction with the glamorous Niner cheerleaders (future actress Teri Hatcher was one of them—more on her later), and the crowd experience becomes warm, exciting, and fun. The fans were extremely knowledgeable of the game, too, and not inclined to cause trouble. They unequivocally loved their team even through all the many down years they endured.

Enthused as they were, by the time I arrived, the fans were growing more and more weary of losing. Evoking a hint of gloom that reminded me of the old Credence Clearwater Revival song "A Bad Moon Rising," the 49er Faithful were sick to death of the losing epidemic. A friend of mine, Bob Halstead, moaned at one of our lunches, "Enduring losing seasons seven out of the last eight years was too much. The Forty-Fucking-Niners better have a winning season."

Football endures for many reasons, but mainly it's because of its simplicity. You win or you lose. You're happy or you're pissed off. You hear a lifetime of tired clichés such as, "It's not whether you win or lose but how you play the game," or "the score's not important—we learned a lot from our loss." But deep inside, every sports fan knows that's bullshit. You win or you lose. And everyone hates to lose. Everything surrounding football is affected by this one simple fact.

Our team outscored the Chicago Bears in my inaugural game, but those Forty-Effin-Niners were blown out by a weak Atlanta team the very next week. After that, the atmosphere soured and fast. Negativity suddenly reigned, and the odds of even having a winning season were long.

CHAPTER 7

LONG ODDS

EL CAPITÁN ORDERED us to attend each game hours in advance. Like everything else around here, we had no clue why. So clever Gunner, Tall Brad, and I would sit in this cheesy windowless War Room, which begged for a paint job. I'd like to meet the guy or gal who said, "Pea green. Let's paint these walls pea green."

Gunner was snapping out. Maybe it was from the coffee served here, so strong you could stand a fork in it. Gunner's a native San Franciscan and still lives where he was raised, in the glitzy Pacific Heights section. He's obviously not here for the money. So much energy bottled up inside of Gunner, he vibrated like one of those egg timers when they hit the three-minute mark. Dude no longer sucked on toothpicks but instead elevated his hand-to-mouth habit by eating an entire pack of Dentine gum in one sitting.

"I've never seen anyone else do that."

"What? Eat a pack of gum? Lots of people do it."

"No, they don't."

Gunner owned a continuous smirk, whether mad or happy and, as I mentioned, wore his security cap down too low. You could barely make out his darting, intense green eyes under the shadow from the brim of the cap. The little ball of energy was always with the chewing. Without gum, he attacked his nails ferociously, nails bitten to the quick.

"Since we're going through another horrific season," he said, "I should at least be down on the field—like you. You gotta be doing some serious brown-nosing to El Capitán to score such a plum assignment. Some of us have been here longer."

"They say jealousy is the strongest of emotions. You're as green as these walls, my friend. Even your eyes are green."

"I'm not jealous of you."

"Yeah, you are. If not, why you keep bringing it up?"

He only glared at me. Guess he took that as an insult. I could tell by his sneer that rich boy's accustomed to getting his way. He was sizing me up. If it comes down to it, I can easily take him. He wouldn't stand a chance.

Tall Brad? Now that might be another story. Resembling a big kid, he backs Gunner on all matters. Athletic build, yes, but his protuberant jaw would make a nice target. I wonder if he uses those long arms to jab. On second thought, I'd probably tackle him to start the brawl. Remove his height advantage immediately.

I can count on my balls how many times El Capitán has even spoken to me. Even then, it was just because I got in trouble with this polyester uniform. Truth is, I have no idea why I got the bench assignment. But to keep the peace, I figured I'd try changing the subject, so I threw out, "Furthermore, I don't think the Niners suck as much as everyone's sayin'."

Of course, Tall Brad, who grew up in the gritty East Bay town of Hayward, had to chip in his two cents.

"You serious? First, the Forty-Fuckin-Niners lost the big final preseason game to their cross-Bay Area rivals, the Raiders, 21–7 which sucked. Now, they start this season with one lousy win against three losses after getting pulverized 34–17 by a terrible team, the Atlanta Falcons. They don't suck? You kiddin' me?"

Gunner said, "Brad's right." Newspapers were always strewn about in the War Room. He read aloud from today's *Chron*: "The 49ers have lost three of their last four games. Everyone's questioning this new supposedly Brainiac coach, Bill Walsh Jr. Why would new owner Eddie DeBartolo Jr. hire an untested, rookie coach from the college ranks, from Stanford no less? Not exactly a college powerhouse. Why did this inexperienced coach then immediately overhaul the entire secondary with rookies such as Ronnie Lott and Eric Wright? That's an NFL first. They'll get lit up. What-on-earth he sees in his new starting quarterback, this skinny, overmatched kid out of Pennsylvania named

Joe Montana was beyond most sportswriter's imagination. On the field, Montana resembles a teenager whose date stood him up for the prom."

Brad chipped in, holding a sports magazine with the creative name, *Sports*, the negativity rising to a new level. Other dweeb guards stood around, listening. "Other sports writers were even more vicious," Brad said and then read aloud: "Coach Walsh is an idiot and needs to be fired. He had a proven, veteran quarterback, Steve DeBerg, who did well last year. Now he favors Joe Montana? Walsh a brainy coach? Ha. If so, why did he turn the entire defense this year over to some cast-off maniac/ renegade named Jack "Hacksaw" Reynolds? Mr. Reynolds earned his nickname for hacksawing a car in half; frustrated his team, the Tennessee Volunteers, lost one single game, for God's sake."

Another beat writer demanded Walsh's head for reasons such as these but especially for "incorporating some bizarre new strategy called the West Coast Offense. It would never, ever, work at the NFL level. It's centered around short little passes. It's used to set up the run. Hello? You know why the Raiders won the Super Bowl last year? Vertical passing, long bombs down the field, that's how. First, establish the running game. Then go deep and over the top. Vertical passing. Our *college* coach is the complete opposite."

"Here's a New York paper, 'Opposing pass receivers staged track meets last season in the secondary defense of the San Francisco 49ers. As a consequence, the Niners turned to three untested rookies? Strange.'"

Las Vegas agreed. They had the Niners as low as low gets: 100–1 odds to make the Super Bowl. In fact, the 49ers and the word *Super Bowl* in the same sentence seemed ridiculous. I slipped out the side door unnoticed. The War Room turned into a bunch of red glowering devils crowding around the bright red boiling pot of goo, shoving in body parts and cursing toward the high heavens in a fit of negative rage. Time to bail.

Walking toward the field, I noticed how the dark clouds hovered around Candlestick Park figuratively and literally. The other guards walked around the Niner fans with their heads down, afraid of setting someone off. Going into the fourth game of the season against the lowly Saints, the Niners offense ranked dead last. From my spot behind the bench, I looked up at the angry crowd and wondered, *Can a guy reach us with a ketchup bottle? Or a battery?*

Because I came from an economically depressed backwater mining town, I formed a superpower many others did not possess. Unlike Gunner, who felt entitled from growing up with wealth, I always found something positive inside a disaster. Where others saw junkyards, I saw a playground. Always found a way to make lemonade from the proverbial lemon. When nothing was happening, I learned how to make something happen. This'll be no different and way better than moping around about 'how the hell could she leave me for another man?' kind of stuff. Although the moment I wasn't busy, I'd scold myself with "the greatest thing ever to happen to you and you blew it."

Besides, during the game, I started getting off on this new West Coast Offense. Yeah, it's taking several years to gel. Yeah, yeah, today's game was against the lowly Saints. Yeah, yeah, yeah, by fumbling the ball four times, they allowed the bottom-dwelling Niners to win ugly. However, I sensed genuine potential.

I converted my dad, also called Rick, into a 49ers fan. He got such a kick out of seeing me on television during the games. I could care less about TV in those days but liked how he of the TV generation enjoyed that. Here's a shot of a security guard, upper right-hand corner, wondering who Joe's talking to on the phone.

Then I walked back over to the other side of the bench to see what R. C. wanted to show me. He saw something no one else did.

CHAPTER 8

R. C. CAN SEE

F ROM MY REGULAR spot nestled between R. C. Owens and the always-hysterical Bob Sarlatte, I looked up at the crowd. They seemed fine.

"Here it comes again," R. C. said. It was funny always hearing his voice coming from so far above the clouds. "Watch for it."

I checked out the Niner offense on the fifty, a mere few yards away, hearing Joe barking out the cadences. Watching the quickness of these athletes this close, well, as I said before, even non-football fans would be in awe. Never gets old.

R. C. could really *see* and showed me what to watch for regarding this new innovative offense. He was figuring out the new West Coast Offense as well but was much further along, saying it would evolve into a precision machine. I preferred hanging with positive-thinking people like this over my vitriol-spewing fellow guards. Although in their defense, rooting for the hapless Niners throughout their lifetimes left them as jilted as, well, me, after learning Joanne dumped my ass for another man.

We watched as my fellow Pennsylvanian, Joe Montana, dropped back quickly—exactly seven steps, precisely ten yards—did two crow hops forward and fired. This became Montana's muscle-memorized MO for years to come. He drilled a bullet to a completely vacant spot on his left side, eleven yards downfield *even though no one was there.* The ball skipped off the turf.

"What the hell, R. C.? Why's he doing that? It's driving everyone nuts? Hurling balls into Candlestick's infield dirt with no receivers in sight looks bad and is why everyone's pissed off."

The offense again failed to convert on third down. As they came off the field, the Forty-Niner Faithful booed lustfully. Our offense simply did not work. Another dreadful season was upon them and excoriating even the most patient of fans.

R. C. flashed his pearly whites, grinning broadly. "Man, I wish I was a receiver in this offense." He started snapping those extraordinary long fingers you see lifetime wide receivers having. "You see, it's all timing, man—and rhythm, a rhythm that takes a long time to perfect. A receiver gots to be heading to that spot *before* Joe throws. A cornerback maybe holds the receiver up at the line of scrimmage, see? Makin' the receiver gettin' there late. Or if not held up, the receiver may get there too early. His route is now past that precise point. You know what I'm sayin'? But they're working it out." He reached down and rubbed the top of my cap. "I see where this is goin'."

Wish I did. To me, it looked like it just flat out wasn't working.

"Precision takes time to master," he echoed, a beacon of light among the rabble.

Next home game, R. C. smacked me on the side again to watch.

"Oh, sorry, R. C. I was watching the crowd a moment, my bad."

The Niners had another third and long, an obvious passing situation. This time, dropping back, Joe looked off the defenders as usual. He was going to pass toward the right side, the opposite side of the field where obviously his receivers ran. Then suddenly, Joe turned in the *completely opposite direction* toward us.

First Dwight Clark and then, on the very next play, Freddie Solomon suddenly appeared out of nowhere, magically, in that *exact* spot. These receivers ran short, crisp yardage routes, looked up *only* when arriving at this fixed spot above, turned, and saw the ball—*already in the air.* They'd catch the ball *in stride* and run for another twenty-yard gain.

More and more, the receivers began arriving at the spot Joe threw his bullets, making the catch and running for more yardage. They racked up massive receiving yardage *after* snagging his spiral. Soon as the defense doubled up on these wide receivers, Joe would hit halfbacks now running pass routes. Then Joe started adding strategic strikes to a tight end to his arsenal. Now, finally, the offense clicked.

Previously, NFL receivers would run, let's say, a buttonhook. They'd get open, catch the pass, but since they were standing flat-footed after the catch, they'd get mowed down on the spot. Not in this new West Coast Offense. Joe's passes never slowed down, just got redirected once they hit the hands of his receivers who in turn carried the rock downfield.

The Niners used this short passing scheme to move the ball like a running team. Previously in the NFL, it was run on first down, run on second down, and if needed, pass on third to pick up the first.

Walsh changed all that. He threw on any down, short precision pops, and not only to wide receivers but to halfbacks and even fullbacks. After the defense adjusted to these short passing schemes, Walsh would ram the ball down their throats by unleashing a relentless running attack.

The West Coast Offense was new, imaginative, dynamic, and fun. Defenses around the league were ill-equipped to stop it, a new phenomenon that simply took nearly two years to develop. Coach Walsh[3] created an ingenious offense so precise that it couldn't be stopped when executed perfectly.

One side effect, however: Walsh became ob*sessed* with *always* executing perfectly. "It would grind on him," says longtime friend Dick Vermeil.

The two most misunderstood facts of the West Coast Offense were this: it's 60 percent running plays. Montana looked like he was dropping back to pass and inadvertently hand it off. Not a draw play but a new creative long handoff.

The defenses, to reiterate, would no sooner start dropping back linebackers ten yards to defend these short passes when Walsh would

---

3   Bill Walsh Jr. was head coach of Stanford for just two seasons before Eddie DeBartolo chose him to run the mediocre, 2–14 Forty-Effin-Niners in 1979. Although they repeated this 2–14 season, Coach Walsh got the entire organization to buy into his philosophy, which included the West Coast Offense. He earned three Super Bowl rings during his tenure from '79 until '88, and his team won a fourth the year he retired. In both '81 and '84, he earned NFL Coach of the Year honors and is in the Pro Football Hall of Fame.

send a Ricky Patton, a Bill Ring, or later, a Roger Craig, high-stepping up the middle for a big gain. The passing game set up the running game. Later, once Walsh firmly established the running game, they would then run play-action fakes—meaning, fake the run. When they bit on the fake, Joe would finally heave the long vertical bombs, which provided the highlight clips for TV.

Another unknown fact as this offense evolved: the receivers had flexibility. If a defender covered their spot or if they *were* held up and couldn't get there in time, they'd run their secondary route to a different spot. Joe, Coach Walsh's prized disciple, had the vision to anticipate the receiver's changes on the go. His pinpoint passes to a previously covered wide receiver became the stuff of legend.

This new offense was all about ball control. Keeping the other team's offense off the field while forcing their defense into exhaustion. The old adage "The best defense is a good offense" was apropos.

However, an even bigger improvement than the offense this season was the defense, which *had* been giving up more points than any other team in the league. Hacksaw Reynolds,[4] once again the polar opposite of his typecast public persona as the wild man from Borneo, brought intelligence and commitment to the D, a maniac on the field and often off (he went through thirteen hacksaw blades that day). The unknown truth was he owned a shoebox full of index cards filled with notes taken watching game film or meetings. He was a true scholar of the game.

This defense significantly improved further when San Francisco traded a draft pick for Fred Dean. Fred became the game's premier pass rusher and provided much-needed veteran leadership on the extremely young team. Signs in the stands proudly proclaimed "Dean-fense" because of Dean's relentless pass-rushing ability.

---

4   Jack Reynolds, a first-round draft pick out of Tennessee, starred for the rival LA Rams for eleven seasons before Coach Walsh brought him over to provide leadership to the young untested defense. Hacksaw made two Pro Bowl teams and would go on to earn two Super Bowl rings in four seasons with the upstart 49ers.

Fred Dean[5] was a natural. I never told anyone about his smoking. Not even Gunner nor Brad. Crazy as it sounds, many times rather than working out with his team before a game during the drills, I'd find Dean smoking in one of the many little hideaways, nestled within the Stick, like in one of the tunnels. Few things in life looked stranger than a giant lineman wearing pads, lying on his back on a bench, and blowing rings of smoke from puffing on a cigarette. Seeing a professional athlete smoking would be shocking unto itself but while in full uniform? I kept my mouth shut as tight as a second coat of paint, practicing my internal motto: "Remain invisible at all times." Fortunately, a security guard easily does this by simply remaining quiet.

Fred Dean loved taking long drags on his cigarettes and watching his exhaled smoke drift away. While his teammates worked up a pregame sweat on the field, I figured on giving the future Hall of Famer a little company. Relaxed as always, lying on a bench, he blew smoke through the gap between two front teeth and asked, "Let me axe you sumthin'. Know why I'm layin' here?"

"No, how come?" I nervously looked around. We should never be seen speaking to players unless it was for security reasons, which was never.

He said, "I got this strange urge to work out. So I'm layin' down till it passes."

That cracked me up. Fred continued, "Why wear myself out? What I gots to do today is easy."

"How's that?"

"I just gotta get the guy in front of me outta the way. Then go chase me some slow-ass quarterback. Wanna know hows I got so good at chasin' down these quarterbacks?"

---

5   Dean was drafted in the second round by the San Diego Chargers after an outstanding career at Louisiana Tech University. A First Team All Pro, Dean constantly led the league in sacks. In '81 Dean joined the 49ers. In '83 his 17.5 sacks and six-in-one game became new NFL records. He owns two Super Bowl rings. Dean was inducted into both the collegiate and the NFL Hall of Fame.

"Sure," I replied, appreciating this guy's wit and humor along with how Coach Walsh was a genius to pick this natural talent up from San Diego earlier in the year for a song and a dance.

"Chasin' them wild-ass rabbits back home in Ruston, Lou-eaze-ee-anna is how. I'd catch'em too. Best drill you can ever run, and I never even knew it at the time."

"You're too much," I said shaking my head while walking away.

Dean and Hacksaw Reynolds plus Dwight Hicks and his Hot Licks, who were the other three rookie defensive backs including future Hall of Famer Ronnie Lott,[6] led an amazing resurrection to the unexpectedly now-formidable "Dean-fense." The crowd chanted "Dean-fense" all season long.

Something big was a-brewin'. Something historical.

---

6   Ronnie, an All-American out of USC, won a National Championship (1978) and played fourteen seasons in the NFL. Recognized as perhaps the best safety of all time, he was elected into the Hall of Fame in 2000. Famous for his hard-hitting style of play, he earned four Super Bowl rings with the Niners. He made First Team All-Pro a stunning eight seasons and was selected into the NFL's All-Decade Team in both the 1980s *and* the 1990s.

CHAPTER 9

THE HISTORICAL 1981 NFC CHAMPIONSHIP GAME

I STORMED INTO EL Capitán's office, clicked my heels together loudly, Roman-saluted him and loudly proclaimed, "Sir, I brought the team good luck, sir."

He grunted, looked up at me with pure disgust, shook his head, and looked back down at his deskwork.

"Last year, my lord, I went to every Raiders home game plus the AFC Championship game. They won the entire Super Bowl. One year later, my extraordinary good luck will do the same for your team, sire."

"Thank you," he said, thumping and straightening a stack of paper. He ignored me as usual. What did my comedic attempts have to do with his running the security business?

I went into the War Room and read in the *Chron*, "Walsh had accomplished something no coach had ever done: conquered the game itself."

The unheralded young San Francisco Forty-Niners *shocked* the league—if there were a stronger verb, I'd use it. Astonished the league maybe? They won fifteen of their last sixteen games, finishing the year at 16–3 in my inaugural season as a security guard and earning their best record in franchise history. At a time when my luck was running poorly no less.

Riding a crest of momentum and with the City in a frenzy like a rabid direwolf foaming at the mouth, the Niners somehow plopped into the NFC Championship game versus their hated rivals, the heavily favored, all-powerful Dallas Cowboys.

Dallas recently proclaimed themselves America's Team, which made Niner fans loathe them that much more. Dallas was in the playoffs for the fifteenth time in the last sixteen seasons and consisted of stone-hardened veterans. Already in four Super Bowls, they were poised to crush these upstarts from the left coast.

Dallas was in the Niners psyche like you would not believe. In the modern history of the 49ers, they only made the playoffs a paltry three times, all in a row, '70, '71, and '72. All three seasons, their same nemesis, the Dallas Cowboys, crushed any postseason dreams of the John Brodie–led 49ers and their fans. The last time, the Cowboys were losing 28–13 in the fourth quarter, and San Francisco thought they would finally break the Cowboy hex. Instead, Roger Staubach, the original Captain Comeback years before Montana, led an improbable, miraculous comeback—including covering a crazy onside kick with under a minute to play—to crush the 49ers' dreams.

The self-proclaimed America's Team pantsed the Niners the two previous seasons as well, including obliterating them last year, 59–14. It was as physical and as thorough a beating as one team could possibly administer upon another. They took the Niners out to the woodshed.

As I walked from the War Room toward the field past the stands, I spotted the ten-gallon Cowboy hats calling us out. "Y'all Niners fans are our bitches. We'll soon be ridin' all y'all's asses. Giddyup, boy."

They were ratcheting up the pure, unadulterated hatred. The Lone Star flag flew around Candlestick. Fights were most definitely a-brewin'. Cowardly, I hustled down to my spot, away from maniac fans decked out in war paint. What if I were forced to do something resembling work and ruin my perfect record?

The Cowboys, like cocky roosters, strolled out onto the field for their pregame drills. Usually, a team jogs out for their drills. These guys ambled out, chests puffed out like robin redbreasts, looking around the stadium they have owned forever. America's Team waved, inciting more boos. The Dallas Cowboys rode the high horse coming into San Francisco. Their starters shut out the Buccaneers 38–0 in the second round of the playoffs and spent the latter part of that game joking around on the bench while the subs mopped the field with Tampa Bay, keeping the shutout intact.

The gamblers wagered the smart money heavily on the Cowboys and their famous Doomsday Defense. But Niner Nation saw this game as destiny. Why else would the Niners' first ever trip to the Super Bowl have devil incarnates as their final hurdle?

I got to my spot and, man, talk about gravitas. Bob Sarlatte raised his eyebrows high. He hugged himself while shaking from side to side. "Even the comedians are serious today," he said.

"We have to win." I gave my creative response.

"I just don't want to see us get embarrassed," he rationalized.

Screw that. We play to win. I hiked around the sidelines and captured the moment doing a 360, looking around the stadium. My god, you could cut the tension down here with a hacksaw.

No one could believe this team, nothing more than ragtag misfits and rookies a few months ago, now faced the powerful preseason Super Bowl–favorite Dallas Cowboy team in, of all places, the 1981 NFC Championship.

I'll never forget how that field shook when the opening kickoff occurred. At this point, I no longer even bothered facing the crowd. I just watched the game and dialed into the goings-on at the bench. My jacket blared SECURITY across my back, so I rationalized that counted for something. I'm sure someone like jealous Gunner reported my ass to El Capitán by now, so this would be my final season anyway. May as well enjoy it while I can.

Game time.

You knew immediately from the high-intensity level of play that this game was destined to become an all-time classic. Dallas led 10–7 after the first quarter, but the 49ers proved they could hang in there. They were not going to get blown off the field this time as widely expected.

Dallas's Doomsday Defense caused *six* Niner turnovers this game, including three interceptions of Joe Montana. Lesser quarterbacks would have become frustrated, but as we could all see, Joe remained cool.

The main man, a.k.a. Joe Cool, projected an image throughout of the quiet Gary Cooper-esque leader on the field. Ha. Ha. Good one. Insiders knew this couldn't be further from the truth.

I loved how Joe Cool talked smack during each game as was his competitive nature. As the NFC Championship battle progressed, Keith Fahnhorst, the Niners' six-foot-six behemoth offensive tackle, got in Joe's face when he sat down on the bench—and yes, players screaming at fellow players were not uncommon.

Keith yelled at our QB in his first full season as the starter and in his first championship game. "Settle down, Joe. You're getting them all worked up out there. They're taking it out on me!"

I knew to what he referred. When Dallas's Harvey Martin sacked Joe in the third quarter, Harvey bent over a crumpled-up Montana lying on the ground like Beetle Baily after Sarge beat him up in the iconic comic strip. Martin trash-talked him, saying, "I *will* be back."

Joe got up, brushed himself off, and replied, "I certainly hope so—I was beginning to think you weren't even in the game." OOOFAH! Martin was livid. Who cared? Joe gave it right back.

Classic stuff. I wrote that one down alongside other razor-sharp barbs from Coach Walsh. Coach blasted anyone underachieving. Real zingers.

Here's one example. One player screwed up, ran off the field, and said, "Sorry, Coach, my mistake."

"No, no, no, don't worry," Coach replied. "It's entirely my fault—for even putting you *in* the game."

During the Civil War, the bloodiest battles occurred in U.S. history at the Gettysburg Wheatfield. The nineteen-acre field of wheat changed hands six times during one single battle.

On this hundred-yard field, the lead also exchanged hands a stunning six times in the single battle. The teams were two heavyweights in the ring, exchanging powerful blows. This was going to go down as one of the greatest championship games of all time.

Then it happened. The moment. Forever frozen in time.

Trailing 27–21, with only 4:51 remaining, the game nearly over, San Francisco had to begin their final drive from inside their eleven-yard line under the shadows of their own goal posts. R. C. Owens, because he was one of them, an official 49er player, could talk to them during the battle, unlike Bob S. and me. During the season, R. C. would often saunter over to the play-calling huddles on the sideline, come back, and give Bob and me the G2.

"We're gonna run it down the field using sweeps," R. C. said.

"Wha? Interesting. Bet everyone's thinking Joe's going to throw short passes," Bob replied.

The Doomsday Defense walked onto the field to put an end to these upstarts from the West Coast once and for all. Coach Walsh knew the Doomsday Defense would drop back to stop these short passes. They put an extra man back. So, Walsh cleverly ran sweeps around the corners for the first time all game.

The Cowboys quickly caught on. On a crucial third down, they disguised their coverage then sprinted to the corner to stop the sweep heading in that direction. The Cowboys set the trap. But get this: Walsh called a risky double reverse using Freddie Solomon, his wide receiver, catching the Cowboys flat-footed. The drive continued. SF was on the move for now.

One fumble, one more turnover—after all, the Niners already had six. Thus, one more and the Cowboys would emerge victoriously. But Joe Cool, man, he was elusive—magic even. He scrambled around and, in between the sweeps, threw clutch, *clutch* passes. The master miraculously marched men all the way down to the Dallas six-yard line. No one could believe it.

San Fran needed a touchdown. Dallas prevented this on the first two attempts. One more stop by the Doomsday Defense would force a pressurized fourth down. This was it, the moment.

The 49ers faced third down and three, with fifty-eight frantic, frenzied, forever Forty-fucken'-Niner seconds left in the game. There was so much bedlam on the field, it was the perfect time for me to surrender any guise of acting as if I was watching a crowd gone bananas. All eyes were, duh, on the field. As if checking something out, I pressed hard on my imaginary earpiece and slithered clandestinely toward the final play. However, there wasn't any need for secrecy. As always, I was as invisible as the white yard line markers. Everyone zoned in. All you could hear was that one constant scream shaking the Stick to its 1960-built metal structures. So loud it became eerily quiet if that makes any sense.

The press, former players with VIP passes, officials, totally random people with no passes whom I should have been asking, "How in the hell did you get down here?" all crept down the sidelines to get near the action in the corner of the end zone to catch the thrilling end of this drive—the final play, the climax.

It looked like an encore at a Led Zeppelin concert when everyone bolts from their seats and crushes down front to dance before the stage. It was even worse than the policeman's ball when somebody inevitably announces, "The doughnuts have arrived!"

I got down there joining the sharp-elbowed young shooters. It was jam-packed. Using my ability to say "Please stand back," I skootched in front of the pack. They thought I was legit. Turning my back to the mob, extending my arms, I acted as if I had taken charge of holding the mob back. Man, it was even louder down here. I hoped there wasn't an earthquake happening because that's how it felt.

In fact, Montana couldn't hear his own signals from the sidelines because of the ear-splitting noise. He darted to the sidelines to get the call. Coach Walsh told him, *"Red Right Tight, Sprint Right."*

Montana slipped under center. Joe Cool calmly looked left then right. Ho-hum, he's slowing the game down again. He called the play, and the intensity in the park elevated to maximum levels. He took the snap. Sprinted right, toward us. I forgot to breathe. He was coming right at me.

Freddie Solomon, the intended receiver cut right too, running parallel to Joe. This same play produced a TD earlier. The Cowboys' coach, Tom Landry, expected this. His team, two plays removed from making their sixth Super Bowl appearance, covered Freddie like a wet blanket, got in his way until he slipped. He went down. Shoot. The play's busted.

Since Joe's protection also sprinted right, three massive Cowboy defenders, unblocked, flanked behind the sprinting blocking scheme.

They fiercely descended upon Joe. He improvised, ran toward the out-of-bounds marker, extending the busted play. Joe needed to buy time, force a plan B, and prevent himself from getting creamed.

Joe ran out of room. He stopped before going out of bounds. Oh no! The big three defenders rushed him like an oncoming runaway train ready to slam him into the opposite end of the universe.

Joe Cool quickly backpedaled. He pump-faked. Instinctively, the three Cowboys jumped up to block his pass, especially Ed "Too Tall" Jones who was closest. Too Tall leaped upward, his six-foot-nine-inch frame ten feet high with his extended arms blocking Joe's view. The other two, Larry Bethea and D. Lewis, did the same.

When Too Tall descended, Joe lofted a pass over Too Tall's head, out of the end zone, thus not losing yardage. He'd still have a fourth down. But wait. Hold on. A miracle. A good old-fashioned freakin' miracle.

Out of nowhere, in the middle of the mingled herd, Dwight Clark suddenly leaped high from the extreme back of the end zone. He pierced the lower part of the ball heading out of bounds with his fingertips. He somehow caught it, gripped it, landed, spiked it, and jogged off the field, never breaking stride. Dude acted like it was just another day at the office. For one shining moment, the longest second ever, the entire place went stone silent. I mean, nothing.

But then . . . *KA-BOOM!* The place exploded as if an atomic bomb detonated.

Niners win.

I read later that Too Tall sarcastically then said to Joe, "Way to go. You just beat America's Team."

Joe replied, "Then you can sit home with the rest of America and watch us on TV."

Now that's Joe Cool for you and one reason he'll be known as the greatest NFL quarterback of all time.

There was no possible way his best friend, Dwight Clark, could jump that high, but Dwight did. Everyone watching thought Joe threw the ball away at that moment despite what they said later.

Montana later confirmed that he could not see the end zone through the leaping defenders. However, he knew *exactly* where Clark would be. The magic was not only in him blindly putting that ball in the only spot on the field where Dwight could go up to make that catch but also in how Joe floated it there, making it a catchable ball.

Any other QB other than Joe Cool, with all the crazed adrenaline flowing, would've rifled that ball, making it uncatchable. We learned later that Joe, Dwight, and Coach Walsh practiced this little play every single week after the regular practice ended—just in case. A worst-case scenario type of play.

"The irony in it," Coach Walsh later said, "was that the play never worked in practice despite there being no pressure. Never. Yet on the biggest stage in NFL history, Joe and Dwight nailed it to perfection."

Everyone celebrated to the max and beyond. All the players mobbed Dwight Clark on our sideline, but not Joe Cool. I figured maybe I should finally do something and pull Joe out from the pile of Niners so he doesn't get crushed. After all, Joe's not a big guy. But holy hell,

Did I spot him jogging across the field to—of all places—the Cowboys sideline? Are you kidding me? Why?

Not till later did I learn he got in the face of Too Tall Jones, pointed at him, and trash-talked him. Look at the videos; you'll never see Joe in there celebrating with his teammates. Ha. Like I said, that's the whole Joe mojo show no one knows—a competitive trash talker. So completely different from his persona—like so many others once you get to know them.

Like Joe, I didn't celebrate the *catch* like everyone else either. The lieutenant, Father Goose, out of nowhere, grabbed me by both shoulders, spun me around, and got in my face. Damn. Here it comes. "What the hell you doing down here? You crazy? Hand in your badge. You're fired."

But that's not what he said. Instead, all excited, he spits all over my face and, in a high-pitched voice, screamed. Like I said, these guys were way too into it. He cupped his hands over my left ear, soaking it with spittle while blowing away my cochlea, screaming, "New assignment! We hafta get those fans off the field! Now!"

He pointed to the shirtless barbarians pouring onto the field like victorious Huns during a rape-and-pillage party.

Wiping my ear and face from the salivary onslaught, I barked back, "Well, good luck with that. These people never saw a championship victory for *any* team *ever* in San Francisco in *any* sport."

I looked at the fan-covered field, at the birth of Forty-Niner Fever, and complained, "Can we get the Tasers I've been asking for like the full-time guards got? They're right upstairs. I know where they're at. Then we could run around the field zapping crazed fans zapped on adrenaline."

"Are you insane?" he asked. "Get out there now."

"We'll never get those damn Tasers," I complained. Like everyone else celebrating the first NFC Championship in Niner history, I just ran around the field like a headless chicken on amphetamine. All you could hear was that loud *hiss* from the deafening crowd *"HHHAAAAAAAAHHH"* again, so loud it was quiet. I know, weird.

However, for the first time all season, there was an actual *need* for me to *do* something resembling work. My perfect record shattered.

The NFL Rulebook states, "The home team gets penalized 15 yards for a delay of game if the fans are not contained."

Fifteen yards would be *huge* because—and everyone forgets this little historical tidbit—there were still fifty-one seconds left on the clock after Clark's most famous touchdown catch ever. With America's Team needing a mere field goal to win, the game was *far* from over.

I kept telling the fans, "You're going to cost us a fifteen-yard penalty, so shake your ass and *please* help me get the others off the field."

The fans understood and helped.

Needless to say, the guards of Burns Security rose to the occasion. We successfully herded the proletariat off the turf with*out* the use of Tasers. I assumed someday there would be a group statue of us outside Candlestick Park.

Our feeling of success lasted less than a New York minute. Suddenly, we stood on the sidelines watching in pure, unadulterated horror. Here it comes, the worst moment in the history of sports.

Dallas, a veteran team, had been here before. While everyone else celebrated, they kept their heads down and began a frantic final finish. Holy cow. We celebrated too soon. A sign of immaturity?

Dallas was driving. The Niners went white with worry. Dallas QB, Danny White, suddenly hit Drew Pearson on a crossing pattern. Two Niner defenders collided going for the ball and went down, freeing Pearson. He broke off with nothing between him and glory.

Pearson was on his way for the winning seventy-five-yard score. Dallas will win the game. What a horrendous shocker. *Get the paramedics ready for all the heart attacks coming in the stands. We'll never recover from blowing this. He's going to dart down the field untouched.*

But wait. Rookie Eric Wright ran behind him, our only chance. Go, Eric! He barely managed to shove a single digit in the back of Preston's shoulder pads, yanked, grabbed, and made a game-saving horse-collar tackle at San Francisco's forty-four-yard line.

The teams rushed downfield to the line of scrimmage. They lined up. Danny White looked left, looked right, and took the snap. He dropped back to pass. Make this completion and Dallas would be in field goal range and win.

The Forty-Niner Faithful filled with fear. Their big games always end like this, in heartbreak. Suddenly Joanne, in my head, said, "You must never be happy."

Danny White brought his arm back to throw. This was it. The Niner defense, always scheming, had called a stunt. Lawrence Pillers broke through the line and slapped the ball out of Danny's hand. Jim Stuckey recovered. Just like that, it was over. 49ers win. 49ers win. By a single digit, 28–27. For the first time in franchise history, San Francisco was going to the Super Bowl. The foghorns went off all over the City. *Brvvvvvvvvvv!*

The next day the papers already dubbed the Montana-to-Clark play as the Catch, proclaiming it "the most famous play in San Francisco sports history, now-and-forever."

It brought San Francisco their first championship, for *any* San Francisco team, *ever!* The call "Red Right Tight, Sprint Right" would go on to become the most legendary call in Niner lore.

In fact, if you look at the "official" photos of the Catch, in the lower right-hand corner, you will see a security guard (ta da!) in the classic position: back to the crowd, knees slightly bent, arms extended with hands facing the crowd as if to say "Stay back" yet eyes firmly glued on the game. But here is a shot I have licensed and it's a unique angle of perhaps the greatest play in NFL history.

Please check the Catch out on Youtube.[7] Or simply search for The Catch and Dwight Clark.

To think a nobody like me was just a few yards away from—well, let Dick Schaap, one of our generation's greatest sportswriter explain it, which was reprinted in the *San Francisco Chronicle*'s Green Pages two days later:

> In the history of professional football, there are only a handful of defining plays that have transformed and elevated the sport:
>
> **1958**: When the Baltimore Colts defeated the New York Giants in sudden death overtime in the NFL Championship game. Johnny Unitas handed off to Ameche to win the greatest game ever played—up until that point.
>
> **1967**: The "Ice Bowl." The Green Bay Packers knocked off The Dallas Cowboys for the NFL Championship and a berth in Super Bowl II. On fourth and one, trailing Dallas 17–14, sixteen seconds left in the game, Bart Star coolly

---

7   The Catch: https://www.youtube.com/watch?v=14CKs0rY0jE

followed Jerry Kramer's historical block over Jethro Pugh and squeezed into the end zone to win it on the game's final play.

1968: When the New York Jets beat the Oakland Raiders for the AFL Championship, on a late 4th quarter drive that saw Joe Namath throw a pass that traveled seventy yards into the arms of Don Maynard on the Raider's six-yard line. On the next play, Namath hit Don Maynard for the winning touchdown.

Now there was "The Catch," the perfect end to a perfect drive, engineered by a quarterback who had a touch of Unitas' brashness, Starr's intelligence and Namath's courage. It was, in a very real sense, the play that spawned the legend—of Joe Montana.

Afterward, as I was getting dressed in our civvies, El Capitán summoned a handful of exhausted guards into an office so full of cigarette smoke your eyes screamed in pain. You would think the dictator could at least crack a window.

"Who among you could travel with the team to its first Super Bowl?"

No hesitation from me. No hesitation was my plan going back to my Jim Schock Raider games. "Yes, I'm in." I then asked, "But I forgot since few ever thought we'd ever get this far, which tropical destination will they hold the game at this year? Pasadena, with the fragrant roses and sunny blue skies? The tropical breezes, beaches, and bikinis of Miami?"

The guards laughed when I outlined a curvy beauty. "The tasteful decadence of New Orleans? They always host the Super Bowls at fun-n'-sun places. Where are we going?"

"Siddown," El Capitán commanded in his gravelly voice, continuing his hate for humor. "None of those," El Capitán allowed a sick smile to spread across his crinkly face slowly. The fascist's answer shocked me to my core.

RICK PUCCI

CHAPTER 10

SUPER SUNDAY, MOTOR CITY

"DETROIT!" I STOOD. The Super Bowl's in freakin' Detroit? Are you kidding me?"

"Shuddup," ordered El Capitán, radiating in his polyester ensemble. "It's in the Silver Dome. Today, it's a balmy minus-twenty degrees with the wind chill factor. The forecast calls for worse. Dress warmly." You could almost hear the "bru-ha-ha" sinister laugh.

"That sucks dick," Tall Brad whispered. "Who the hell made *that* decision?"

El Capitán smirked. We were his go-to guys. He knew the crew in blue knew not how to say no, so, we'd go even though this was still my first year. However, I felt like a hardened veteran because of never missing a game.

El Capitán splashed an image up on the screen of the inside of the Silver Dome. He used one of those old-fashioned brown pointers with the black tip. Haven't seen one of those in years, but then again, this organization reveled in low-tech.

"No, not Pasadena, not Miami, not New Orleans. The NFC Champion Forty-Niners are taking on the AFC Champion Cincinnati Bengals in the height of winter in Detroit, Michigan."

He showed us our positions. The fascist enjoys this. Such luck. My first Super Bowl's also the first one ever played in a cold-weather city. Boy, oh boy.

Two weeks later, on Super Sunday, I was rudely awakened. I looked around my cheap hotel room, again with the pea-green walls.

"What? Was this color a trend once?" I said aloud while getting up.

Still hazy, I sat back in my bed looking down at those who awakened me; my two comrades huddled in front of the TV at the base of my bed.

"You up?" Gunner asked.

"I am now."

"Every year they show highlights of previous Super Bowls, so we turned your TV on," Gunner said in that too-early-in-the-morning shrill, annoying voice of his.

However, he was correct. There's Vince Lombardi, the NFL's daddy, and the Pack, winning the first ever Super Bowl. It made us feel we were soon to witness history ourselves. The morning had gravitas. We watched previous pregame Super Bowl activities in lush tropical locations with tanned cheerleaders, beaches, pools, palm trees under blue skies.

I got up then peered outside at the ice bonded to our windows. I turned the heat up inside the unit under the window, which sounded like a buzz saw.

"You guys see these monster icicles out here? One of them falls, they'd pierce a man in half."

"Quiet," Gunner commanded. "Check this out."

Frostbite warnings ominously flashed across the screen. Unlike noble Romans, we came . . . we saw . . . we froze. Soon we will see about the conquering part. And why was Gunner telling *me* to be quiet when he's sitting in *my* room?

"Well, at least you never threw me under the bus, Gunner, as you threatened. I still somehow got the cherry assignment today."

"Yeah, because you're giving El Capitán blow jobs under his desk."

I nailed him good with a pillow. A major pillow fight broke out. We weren't the most mature guards on the team. As usual, Brad took it too far. After Gunner ridiculously slammed him in the face, Brad, who loves to overreact, punched him in the nuts. As I grinned and watched Gunner rolling around in pain, I realized the dork had a point. I'm not *in* with El Capitán at all. He acted like he hated my guts. The few times he spoke to me was always 100 percent business, and I do mean 100 percent. Why he always gave me such plum assignments equated to what Winston Churchill said when describing Russia: "It's a riddle wrapped in a mystery inside an enigma."

Heading into the bathroom for my morning ablutions, I peered at my two friends and shook my head. They finished wrestling but spread sunflower seed shells all over the carpet. Gunner, panting, still chewed crazily, like a man possessed, insisting he gets to punch Brad in the ball sack to be even.

"Why don't you make a mess like that in your own room?" I asked the nervous little prick who just can't stop masticating.

"Our room's too messy, and whadya care? The maid'll clean it."

Then I said no to Brad offering me a toke on the number he had fired up.

"This early in the morning, Brad? Are you kidding me? Egads. But at least now I know why your eyes are always so red. And why you seem to be on a distant planet half the time."

After my shower, I dried my hair to . . . Was it the pleasant morning songs of the North American songbirds chirping outside in the sunlight? No, it was to the hysterical sounds of Brad screaming in pain. Get high and then get your nuts punched in. What idiots.

After Brad recuperated, I tossed a few singles on the dresser for the poor maid stuck with cleaning this dumpster. There were now pillow feathers mixed in with seeds and shells and overturned garbage cans. We escaped downstairs, scarfed waffles and coffee, bundled up, and split to the freezing Silver Dome.

Getting off the bus, we guards quickly realized we wore the worst footwear imaginable: black wingtip shoes with patented leather soles as per our goofy uniform requirements. What a sight that must have been. Security guards taking baby steps and sliding on a glacier of ice leading toward the stadium. I slid the wingtips slowly and deliberately to stay afloat. Whoops! There goes Gunner head over heels. Ha. Good for the little know-it-all prick. Never heard so much cursing.

Under gloomy gray skies, the frigid, whistling wind ripped right through our cheap jackets. The freezing rain sandblasted our faces. The minus twenty-one degrees assured us we were at the coldest Super Bowl for all time. Minus twenty-one! How did the Packers and the Cowboys play in this weather in the Ice Bowl for the NFL Championship? The arctic chill numbed us to the bone.

Inside the Dome, with its plastic synthetic smell, the scene got even stranger.

"Check those out," Gunner pointed toward the roaring sound.

"What are they?" tall Brad asked, stoned out of his gourd.

"Pressurized air blowers keeping the trampoline-like roof up. The game's gonna be played inside a giant hefty bag with huge fans running all game," Gunner said. "They stop blowing, the roof falls and covers us."

Which led to one of my mental takeaways from under this circus tent—the blowing of the women's hair straight up their backsides as they watched the game. Ultra-bizarre.

None of this strangeness, however, could prevent this game from becoming the most viewed telecast of all time—as in *ever*! It was the most watched sporting event in history. Eighty-five million viewers tuned in, making the stunning 49 percent Nielsen rating the highest rated event on record.

My job? Simple: keep an eye on the Niners' bench during Super Bowl XVI. My yearlong acting experience of watching entire games without anyone bothering me over something inane like some security issue should work just fine. I felt lucky hearing what scalpers charged for tickets outside.

Gunner, whose constant complaining finally wormed him on to the other side of the bench, strolled over. "I just heard Coach Walsh dressed up as a bellhop in front of the hotel and greeted the players coming off the bus. He even wrestled with Montana over his bags until Joe recognized him and cracked up."

"That's hysterical. Who said Coach's got no sense of humor? I'm sure that loosened the fellas up."

Tall Brad, who came out of nowhere, added, "That probably loosened the fellas up," then wandered off somewhere into the crowd. Brad was usually taciturn, and when he finally spoke, you could see why. Gunner and I watched him shaking our heads in disbelief.

We watched Detroit's very own Diana Ross belt out the national anthem, and *whoosh*, the game zipped right on by rather quickly.

Coach Walsh's scripted pregame precise plays were effective. His 49ers jumped out to a 20–0 halftime lead behind Joe Montana's heroics of running for a TD and passing for another. The first-year starter appeared to slow the game down to a crawl while everyone one else acted like nervous wrecks.

However, after the University of Michigan's marching band left the field, the second half was another story. The Niners faced a *furi*ous Bengal rally. Cincinnati suddenly had their way with San Francisco's finest and had captured the momentum. I silently strolled over to Gunner who acted all cocky like for finally scoring a bench assignment. I made a few nonsensical pointing gestures with my hand toward the crowd to give the appearance as if we were discussing security issues. As if in a Shakespearean play, Gunner also acted out his part, over dramatically. For some reason, he carried a clipboard with not a single thing on it. Then we got down to brass tacks.

"What the hell?" I asked. "After this miraculous season, we're reverting to the Forty-Fuckin'-Niners?"

"No shit, Dick Tracy." Gunner looked worried. He bet a ton on this game. Dude had a gambling problem. "We're gonna blow the biggest game in franchise history."

"Well, I'm not as negative as you, Gunner, but it's certainly looking that way."

Cincinnati's closer to Detroit than SF. The orange-clad Bengal section outnumbered Niner Nation. They roared when Ken Anderson hit Chris Collingsworth for a forty-nine-yard long bomb to get the Bengals into the red zone once again: first and goal from the five. They had big *mo* on their side.

I looked up at the red-n'-gold Niner Nation section. They looked freaked out. Strolling down the sideline, amazed as usual at my invisibility, I looked around for Father Goose. But he continued his tradition of always completely vanishing during the games. Except for that one time, the Dallas NFC Championship game, when he popped up from a mole hole in the ground and spit all over my face. I wonder where he crawls off to during games.

Everyone sensed this was the denouement of the Super Bowl. Cincy was going to take the lead and win the game.

First down: All-Pro Bengal Pete Johnson smashed his way up the middle, down to the Niner one-yard line.

"All he needed now was one measly yard. This totally sucks," I said to the guy wearing a VIP badge around his neck. He gave me the World War II thousand-yard stare, shocked that a guard could emote words. I got away from him quickly, sneaking down the sideline, putting on my act.

Second down: Johnson burst into the line off tackle. But 49er linebackers, Hacksaw and Dan Bunz, stopped him for a one-yard loss.

Third and goal: two teeny-tiny yards away. Man, was it loud down here. It sounded like a jet's engine roared next to my ear. I checked out the crowd, doing my duty to God and country. They were fine. I turned back to the Super Bowl.

Bengals veteran quarterback, Ken Anderson faked the run. Damn. San Fran fell for the fake. Anderson tossed a swing pass out to the flat to their halfback Charles Alexander. Every Niner fan groaned. Anderson sold the fake. Alexander glided in for the winning touchdown.

But wait. Oh my god! Linebacker Dan Bunz materialized out of thin air! He must have emerged from a portal in space. Dan tackled Alexander right smack literally on the goal line—an absolute picture-perfect tackle.

The ball came down a micro of an inch from the plane of the goal line—a razor-blade's width from pay dirt. Dan Bunz saved the day, another forever 49er moment, setting up the most dramatic play in all of sports: fourth and goal.

Fourth and goal with the Super Bowl on the line.

Eighty-two thousand people stood, cupped their mouths with their hands and primal-screamed. Barbaric. This was it. In one more second, one half of the stadium will be ecstatic. The other half depressed, all in a single moment. I took a massive deep breath, capturing the moment. The Bengals eleven-year veteran quarterback, Ken Anderson, waved his hands up and down to calm everyone, slowing the moment so his linemen could hear the count. He crouched behind the center, looking around.

Anderson barked out the signals. He'll show this upstart punk, Montana, why experience still rules. He dreamed of this moment, playing with the game on the line as a little boy in his backyard in Batavia, a Chicago suburb. He was *soooo* ready.

The Niner white jerseys lined up against the orange Bengal jerseys on the goal line, ready to decide the outcome at the lowest common denominator in the trenches. Tension mounted supreme, sucking all air from the room.

Ken called the play. He took the snap. My ears bled from the noise. I let my breath out, forgetting I had been holding it. They went with their best. Anderson handed it off to his All-Pro fullback Pete Johnson. He crashed into the direct center of the line.

Like a whiter Styrofoam cup placed over an orange burning match, the 49ers snuffed him out, the defensive led by none other than the crazed Hacksaw Reynolds. Everyone thought Hacksaw was an unusual pick by Coach Walsh in the beginning of the year. Criticized him. Ha. Ha. Where were the doomsayers now?

Thus concluded as fine a goal-line stand as the game will ever see. The celebration was *on*. We all hopped around on the sidelines like a prison break. Yeay!

Final score: San Francisco 26, Cincinnati 21. The San Francisco Forty-Niners won their first ever Super Bowl. San Francisco celebrated their first ultimate championship ever in any sport. Joe Montana won the MVP award. I even called Joanne figuring my luck had broken. She never returned my call. Oh well, it's only been a mere five months since we broke up. She'll eventually come around.

I watched the victory parade firsthand from my vantage at Market and Bush Street. The gratifying, glorious gargantuan gilded downtown San Francisco ticker tape parade equated to something you would never ever forget. Business ground to a halt. Streets closed. The tall financial buildings miraculously poured confetti thickly over the motor parade as if from the heavens above. Everyone cheered nonstop. Mere words cannot remotely capture the spirit in the air.

Young couples kissed passionately. Young men bent knees, flashed diamonds and proposed to their sweethearts. Newborn babies, their names coming from members at the same 49ers parade, suckled their mother's breast. Fathers snatched these babies from their feast and held these infants on high to catch a glimpse of the Cittay's conquering heroes. Grown men who followed this team since it originated in 1949 openly wept.

One tall, rail-thin old guy, wearing his best suit for the occasion, looked down upon me. Crying like a sieve, he whimpered, "I never thought I'd live to see this day. And here it is." Goose pimples.

Damn, I wish they had telephones you could carry in your pocket. I would've called the evil woman who dumped me when the season began who always said, "Please, it's only a game."

Is it only a game? Look at the City's heroes riding on the backs of convertibles and inside motorized cable cars, who waved to their adoring throngs. Roman emperors returning from a conquest from the frigid Michigan hinterlands. *Il Magnifico!*

Five famous Forty-Niner fellas chose to attend the parade instead of going to the prestigious Pro Bowl in Hawaii, breaking a rule. Never was this done before. The Pro Bowl's a big deal. The NFL brass fined the five, a tab owner Eddie DeBartolo only too happily paid.

Bodies, as you can see in this photograph—look up at the lamppost—were everywhere. Note Owner Eddie DeBartolo, Mayor Dianne Feinstein, and Coach Bill Walsh leading the cable cars looking like Roman Emperors *returning from another* victorious campaign. The Niners rode behind, many on the country's only moving national landmark, the SF cable cars. January 15, 1982, was certainly a day to remember.

However . . . you'd think they could've spared at least one convertible for us humble security guards so we too could wave to our adoring fans.

I suddenly remembered for a second how low I was after Joanne nuked my weary heart. How low the city was during those rainy, fog-filled, mud-filled, losing-early games, bathing in the daily negative press. Having traveled from there all the way to here, there are no words to describe it, but our mayor did her best.

A proud mayor, crying tears of joy, said in her speech to the masses:

"I became mayor in November of '78 under very difficult circumstances with the assassinations of my predecessor George Moscone and Harvey Milk. There was hatred like I have never seen. San Francisco had some very, very dark days.

"Into this very disparate situation came the Niners and began to win. People took great pride in something going right.

"I can truly say, this first Super Bowl victory united a fractured city. It's a sense of fulfillment in the wake of the assassinations of George Moscone and Harvey Milk. the Niners helped a broken city heal."

So how could you go from here, at the extreme height of the summit, to the deepest low in the valley in a single year? How?

CHAPTER 11

'82: WHAT A DIFFERENCE A YEAR MAKES

1 982. FINALLY REACHING the top of the long outdoor escalator taking me to the top of Candlestick Park, I looked straight east over the bay waters. Screeching seagulls and cotton candy clouds dotted the view from atop the oldest stadium in the NFL, built in 1960. The air was super fresh now that the drenching rains abated, creating a sense of serenity. I could see those badass rain clouds leaving us and hustling down to San Jose to give that dirty city a needed drenching. The protesters grew quiet outside the protective walls, and the usual murmur of the crowd inside the Stick provided the bass.

Last year, I was on one of those clouds, cloud nine. The Niners shocked the sports world, going from perennial doormats to Super Bowl Champions. And who could ever forget the mother of all parades?

Now, not only are the 49ers god-awful again, but instead of watching Super Bowls, I was busy guarding SCABs during a nasty, violent NFL players' strike. And now, I'm about to get fired.

Before entering El Capitán's office way up there, I practiced my speech, "El Capitán, I let you down, blowing my assignment of keeping the guards in line. Truth be told, I only took this job to get close to the action on the field. No need to fire me. I'll resign."

Speaking of clouds, I entered one—a cloud of smoke. I sat across from my boss. Holy cow, what was going on in here? His desk had two ashtrays heaping with disgusting cigarette butts. El Capitán stood. Built like a toothpick, he still managed to look like he lost weight. So skinny in fact, if he covered one eye, he'd look like a needle. When he stood sideways, you couldn't even see him. He fired up a truck driver, an unfiltered Kool, and paced.

I began my memorized resignation soliloquy: *"El Capitán,* I know I let—"

"Quiet." He flashed his palm out. "I talk. You listen." He paced a figure of eight, smoke trailing behind him as if he were a toy train. "Burns Security's struggling. Big time. Another four part-timers quit today. I don't have the budget to bring on any more full-timers. I told those pencil-necked geeks at corporate we're severely understaffed. That's why what happened today happened. It was a disaster, yes, but it could've been worse. A lot worse." His gaze dropped to his perfectly black shiny shoes.

"Jeez," I said. "Doom and gloom and their cousin despair are in the air. Whoever said, 'What a difference a year makes knew what the hell they were talking about.' Last year seems like a dream. Now, the Niners are terrible. The Oakland Raiders, just one year removed from winning the Super Bowl, bailed on us and moved to LA. On top of that, there's this ugly strike. And now you're understaffed. When it rains, it pours."

El Capitán sat with a thud. He said hoarsely, "Our orders: bring these replacement players into the Coliseum each week and feed them to the lions, like today. The press and protesters call them SCABs. Know what a SCAB means?"

"Yeah, stands for 'still can't afford beer.'"

Well, knock me over with a feather. A modern-day miracle—El Capitán smiled. I always thought a smile would crack his cemented face. The square wrinkles covering his cardboard face shifted into lines. The fascist quickly recovered, however, and reverted to his natural scowl. Still, I got off on this guy finally talking man-to-man with me for the first time.

"No, scabs are like this."

Good God. The wirey boss rolled his white polyester shirt sleeve up, past a faded navy anchor tattoo. He pointed to a fluorescent-pink scab on his forearm. I could've puked right there.

"We'll have to keep guarding them each home game until the cows come home and they are hate-*ted*." He rolled his starched, bleached white sleeve back down.

I asked, "Why didn't the cops provide better protection? Their shields barely protected us to start with, but we really got pelted after they retreated."

"The SFPD gets you through the picket line period, end of story. That's where their responsibility ends. It's not to guard nonunion replacement players the cops resent. Keep in mind, they are all *about* unions. They're in a police union themselves."

Great. But no SCABs, no games. Then I'm back perseverating on when JT's coming back into my arms, which she's apparently not. I can't believe it. I need this gig to keep my mind off that pretty soft face, the honey-colored soft hair, the green-emerald eyes highlighted by the rich, dark natural-brown eyebrows, and those tight hugs. You don't know what you got until you lose it. Wish I knew then. It wasn't fair. It was like being given the most delicious dessert you would ever taste in your entire life, but unbeknownst to you, you would never taste it again. She's always one thought away. I looked down at my soaked shoes. What a bummer.

El Capitán peeled his cap off, pushed both his receding hairline and the invisible stress backward. "Veteran guards resigned today. Guarding SCABs was *not* in their best interests. However, where are my new hires? We *are* advertising."

"New hires are rare because probably they thought like I did last year. They assumed there'd be no opportunities for a great job like this. Or they thought this nasty strike'll never end."

El Capitán slid a rough-hewn rock paperweight across his desk. "Keep this."

I grabbed it and read aloud the quote on its face:[8] "In the middle of difficulty lies opportunity"—Albert Einstein.

I thanked him, wondering where he was going with all this—feeling low even though I now know, I won't go. No, I keep this job.

---

8   That same rock lives on my office desk to this day.

"Under normal situations, privates like you take years to get promoted to corporal. But we're hurting. You're going on two years now with experience guarding the bench, plus traveling with the team to the Super Bowl. Well, suddenly and unfortunately, that's a lot."

"Ah, the beauty of attrition or, as Paul McCartney sang, 'Take a sad song and make it better.'"[9]

He despised rock references. "Remember what you tol' me during our initial interview?" he croaked, emitting smoke—smoke that exited his mouth even when he spoke naturally.

"What? That interview lasted ten minutes. I hardly said a thing."

"No. You said you finish everything you started no matter what. Remember? I need that now."

"I drug that ol' corny line out? I don't even remember—"

"You're enthusiastic about your job as well, even during dark times like these."

You mean I'm enthusiastic because of my proximity to the game for free, I thought then thought about something else quickly in case El Capitán was telepathic. Never knew with this guy. He was after all . . . different.

The skeleton jumped up and extended a bony arm toward me. I shook the cold end of it. "You're promoted to sergeant. New responsibilities: You'll guard the main door inside the Niners' locker room immediately. I'll introduce you to the people you'll allow in. Remain invisible among the players once inside unless they ask for something. *Never* let the press in, except for the official postgame interviews. They *must* have credentials no matter what their bullshit story is. You see someone in that sacred inner sanctum you don't recognize, then 'prevent and report.' After the game concludes, you will be assigned a 'private, top secret' assignment each game. Got it? Good. Now. Leave me."

---

9   "Hey Jude," written by Lennon-McCartney, August 1968. Voted by nearly every magazine as one of the greatest songs of all time, it topped the U.S. charts through staggering nine consecutive weeks or most of the summer of '68.

The terrible strike finally ended. Our first home game began late in the season, November 28, 1982. As always before each game, I sat in our windowless cheesy War Room with Gunner and Tall Brad. During the offseason, I shockingly found out these two jamokes were execs like myself. They invited me to a fundraiser Gunner threw in a stunning chandelier-laced, marble-laden mansion in Pacific Heights. They were unrecognizable in their tuxes, which proves this whole security guard experience equated to pure nonreality. These were our alter egos.

Gunner offered me a jawbreaker and fired one into his pie hole. "Well, they're back to being the San Francisco Fucking Forty-Niners after just one season. They're 0–3 and the first team to ever lose to the new LA Raiders."

I accepted his candy. "You stopped chewing entire packs of gum to satisfy your hand-to-mouth obsession?"

"Yeah, my doctor said I was getting TMJ from chewing gum all day. Seeds are too damn messy, so this'll work fine." Next came that mischievous Gunner grin.

He went back to his natural smirk. "The Niners blow this year. They're hung over from their first Super Bowl success."

Brad put his Styrofoam cup down encasing his cheap burnt coffee. I grimaced at the smell as he said, "Everyone's calling last year a fluke."

"Plus, the strike's spread a bad vibe over everything. Players got too greedy. That's what's on the news outlets anyway. You think they're too greedy?" Gunner asked.

"My humble opinion? The average NFL player lasts what? Three seasons? Ninety percent of them sustain lifetime injuries. Why shouldn't they earn as much as possible within their little window of opportunity? Now, for the first time in any sport, not just football mind you, players' contracts are public. They can compare what they're making against similar positions. Hell, they found backups were making more dough than the damn starters. This'll revolutionize sports. But hey, what do I know? We're lucky we didn't catch a battery to the brain, lucky to be alive. Especially you, Brad, could you have run any slower that day?"

"Huh? What day?" he asked.

Gunner said, "What I *do* know is this: give the politically conscious citizens of San Fran a reason to protest, and they'll come out of the woodwork. Last night, for example, dolphin-free tuna protests shut down traffic. I couldn't get home from work."

"Poor baby," Brad said, squeezing Gunner's face until Gunner slapped his hands away saying, "Watch it, asshole." Gunner sat up, and Brad pushed him right back down. Here we go.

El Capitán destroyed our intellectual conversation, sticking his head in, screaming as if he shoved his hand into a pot of boiling water, "They're here! Move it!"

Gunner whipped out the flask. We each took a deep slug as per tradition. After a loud smacking of the lips, we bolted outside to guard the incoming visiting team.

In addition to the fine Irish whiskey, Gunner also had a point. The Niners went 0–5 at home, 3–6 overall, and amazingly, many fans jumped off the bandwagon after the 1982 season concluded. Coach Walsh felt so dismal, he seriously considered retiring.

In fact, 1982 was such an absurd season that Mark Moseley, a freaking placekicker was named the NFL's MVP. He did set records with his 95.2 percent accuracy number and his twenty-three consecutive field goals, but a field-goal kicker as the league's most valuable player? It never happened before or since.

The Montana-to-Clark combo proved to be the only shining light. Dwight earned Player of the Year. Joe set the all-time NFL record with five consecutive three-hundred-yard passing games. One of the youngest teams in the league, the defending champion '81 Niners were simply too young and ill-equipped to handle that much sudden success the previous year. Whoever said nothing spoils success like success knew what they were talking about. San Francisco did not prepare properly for 1982, a disastrous season for the home team.

What El Capitán laid on me next regarding that little top-secret assignment superseded everything.

CHAPTER 12

'83: THE INNER SANCTUM OF AN NFL LOCKER ROOM

WHEN THE '83 season kicked off, my new assignment, guarding the locker room door was ultra-cool. El Capitán's private assignment for me was even cooler. Why? There was a Joe Cool element to it.

After the locker room interviews concluded, my new postgame assignments were unreal: first, here's how El Capitán put it, "Get *Joe Montana* out of the Stick." Unquote.

Traveling through a myriad of tunnels underneath the ancient ballpark, I accompanied Joe and the same fellow who drove him around. Dude always wore mirrored shades, sports coat, and meant nothing but business. A big nameless guy, he looked like an undercover agent with his wavy hair. But he wasn't a big muscle-bound type of guy like you might think of when you hear the word *bodyguard*. More like a dedicated professional escort, let's-get-out-of-here type of guy. He never left Joe's side whenever Joe was off the field, and if given a chance, I'm sure he'd guard him on the field as well. Pretty sure he was packing heat but couldn't say for sure. That bulge could've been a fat wallet. Hey, it's possible. Very dedicated attitude: protect Joe from all things. You can see him on any videotape or photograph showing Joe jogging off the field after another game-ending comeback. Joe flashed his smile and did his patented "quick three-question quick answer" segment to the grabby sideline reporter in the patented interview, and there's the guy on him like white on rice—that's how quickly he attached himself to Joe's side.

You can spot him corralling Joe in this famous television commercial[10] after Joe won the Super Bowl. Initially, everyone thought that was a spontaneous reply, but once the commercial came out, the world knew. You can also see my red security cap twice in this commercial and my hair, but since I cannot prove it, I won't mention it.

Joe, introverted, *despised* dealing with the press or fans. He preferred being left alone after games. Funny thing, Joe never shied away from talking trash to the 300-pound-plus linemen trying to maim him, from providing fiery leadership to his team during game time, nor from his pranks either.

The practical jokes he'd pull during training camp in Rocklin became legendary. Players would travel back and forth to practice along the rural paths from their bunkhouses on bicycles. After a meeting, however, they'd spend fifteen to twenty minutes searching for same bikes up in trees. Trees lined with bicycles being a surreal sight. No sooner would a 300-pound lineman climb a tree and pull his bike out than he would discover it was somebody else's—to roars of laughter. Who was doing this? No one knew. Another Niner mystery—until Joe confessed years later.

Outside the locker rooms and rustic training camps, in social circles or during interviews, Joe would be shy as hell.

Anyway, let's flashback to what it was like back then as per my documentation. Let's slip into present tense. Today's game just ended. There's Joe freakin' Montana and his bodyguard. We're both right on time. Ready? Let's go.

Into this maze we jog, deep inside the bowels of Candlestick Park. Maybe only two other humans in the world know how to navigate this route and not get totally lost. We're off. Follow me through the trainer's room, through the locker room's ancient rust-smelling back door. We pop outside. Good, it's nice outside but already dark—quick pace. We're

---

10   Joe Cool and his personal security guard at the end of his famous "Going to Disneyland" television commercial: https://www.youtube.com/watch?v=sZV1qLRrXcQ

outside only one minute then under the bleachers, now a sharp right into a secret tunnel.

"Watch out for rats," I say to deaf ears. Those two don't even talk to each other. Here's my favorite part. We now traverse through the Stevens's Room; Stevens equals the organization controlling the yellow-clad vendors crawling all over the stadium announcing and selling their wares. They always have this postgame poker party. These guys rack in cash selling beer, hot dogs, sodas, whatnots, and let's not forget that nutritious cotton candy. Then they sit gambling their take of it away. Beautiful.

Passing through their smoky room, we slow down crossing their slippery ashtray of a floor. I'm probably getting irreversible lung damage breathing here. He will say this many words to me throughout my career: zero. We three flee and emerge onto the complete opposite end of the Stick at Gate E. Busses line the street outside, choking the environment by the neck with carbon monoxide. You can taste it, dark gray matter, thick in your mouth as if it were spoiled lunch meat.

There's the black Caddy, spotless and shining in the brilliant moonlight, windows tinted, engine running, ominously waiting. The two men hop in the back. The chauffer slams their door shut and sprints around the car to the driver's side. I slap the large vehicle on its ass as per my custom, and the Caddy whisks superstar and bodyguard away. They simply disappear into the dark San Francisco night. Wow!

I turned back and checked our route. One could easily hide a body along this trail—never to be found. Can I run that as an ad? "Bodies hidden. Two bodies for the price of one, a Saturday night special." Hmmm, might be an entrepreneurial move someday. Or someday, say in the year 2017, the powers that be can set this route up as a tourist attraction, one I'm sure the 49er Faithful would pay a fair price to travel for nostalgic reasons.

Hands on hips, watching Joe drive off into the west, into the always pitch-black dark Candlestick night, I turned around and looked the other way, to the east to capture another moment. This was the only time all day I would be alone.

Outside the stadium, Gate E ends high on a hill, looking out at the bay waters. There was nothing, and I do mean nothing around but the black-as-ink night. Amazing how ominous and dark water appeared at night. Out here, alone, a guy can seriously think, hear his most inner thoughts, just below that busy surface. I dropped my head, inspecting my wingtips.

What were my goals in life? What were my plans now that Joanne . . . See? Aaargh! There it was. Whenever I was alone, instead of thinking profound or creative thoughts, my mind loved to flash images of my lost love. How she changed her hairstyle to bangs perfectly matching her eyebrows. That sweet tone of her skin. Her always-stunning soft hair. How I loved running the backs of my index and middle finger over the cheeks of that face I loved. Truly loved. The fullness of both her radiating smile and that committed hug she presented me after coming home from work each day. She would say she loved smelling the sun on my body during our long hug. I hate my mind for this. Will I never win her back? I heard she's still going out with this yo-yo, the guy in my place. How can she be happier in the arms of another man? What a colossal bummer.

The expansive black hole before me had a gravitational pull, zeroing in on my loneliness. I stood on the edge of a frightening periphery, a black vortex of paranoia and anxiety. I asked God, in whom I trust, "Please cut me a break here." To tell me I didn't blow the only chance I'd ever have at finding true love.

My heart dropped. I was alone. I stood in what seemed like a pitch-black darkroom, running my hands alongside a wall, looking for that switch. As this search to replace her became prolonged, the crazed anxiety deep within me strengthened, the midnight awakenings from a racing heart. I looked upwards. I can only hope.

My mind, feeling sorry for one so damn pathetic, tossed me a lifesaver. *Get busy fast,* it told me. *Now.*

I hustled around the stadium running to good ol' Gate A as fast as the stiff wingtips, not built for speed, would take me.

Each game, I met tall Brad there staring at his gargantuan Mickey Mouse watch. I spotted the massive, boisterous mob and, like a ten-year-old, dove into a summer pool.

"Nine more minutes," Brad warned, siding up.

Then we started the same old process: pulling Dwight Clark, with his bangs, boyish good looks, and charms, away from his adoring mob and nearly all young ladies.

The nine minutes passed. Following Brad in deeper, he turned to me while clearing a path through the mob. I felt like a Colombian with a machete clearing a path through the Amazon rainforest toward the river.

"Dwight's the polar opposite of his roommate and best buddy Joe. Dwight plunges deep into the heart of this crowd after every single game."

Duh. Brad loves making the obvious crystal clear. I'm with him each time doing this. Does he not remember? I looked into the center of the mob. Dwight's slapping signatures on photos of *The Catch*. He posed for photos, hugs, and autographed stuff nonstop until Brad and I finally grab one arm each and literally drag him back to the lockers.

"Dwight, please sign one more for my daughter—she loves you."

"Step back, buddy," I would say to the guy with a high probability of obtaining the signature for himself.

Dwight loved being with his adoring fans—such a personable star, autographing everything imaginable. Last week, he signed a silicon-enhanced tit with a black felt pen. That one I won't soon forget. He enjoyed talking about his great season last year, his famous catch highlighted on every magazine cover the previous year, 1981. In 1982, *Sports Illustrated* honored him with their Player of the Year award. Dwight Clark led the entire league with sixty receptions and was on his way to break every single-season mark, was at his All-Pro peak when the stupid strike hit. A fan favorite. You simply could not come up with a better guy.

The following week, I sat on my stool realizing I *loved* working inside the locker room, especially keeping the bastards and the paparazzi out during the NFL-mandated press conferences. I heard a knock, opened the door albeit slightly. It was Carmen Policy, VP and team counsel. "Please come in, sir."

Later, a booming knock I recognized immediately, owner Eddie DeBartolo Jr. who stormed right in. Five minutes later, another, a lighter knock. A gorgeous female reporter who started lightly rubbing just the hair on my forearm up and down.

"I need just five minutes with Dwight for KCBS. I'll make it up to you later," she purred.

I checked her out. This probably worked well for her. Especially on us desperate souls.

"Sorry. It's not even remotely possible," I said, rather unfortunately. Then I recounted all the women this uniformed job had brought me thus far. Yeah, that'd be zero. But there was always hope. Tall Brad I knew used his uniform quite well with the ladies, however. I'll give him that. Or it could be his boyish-looking charms. Or his *laissez-faire* attitude. Or that they just used the ol' chap to get into the sold-out games for free. Whatever it was, I shan't be jealous. But I needed to set up a sit-down with Joanne—and fast.

In the meantime, being in there with NFL players before the games was surreal. I used my other secret superpower, invisibility, to my advantage. I was not supposed to be walking around among the players, just guarding the door each week. However, like Jack's beanstalk, my boldness grew. As I said, security guards were completely obscured by players and personnel, adorned in familiar traditional uniforms—a part of the landscape. You wouldn't believe what people discussed right in front of us. We were silent. We weren't deaf.

I prowled around, always with the looking-around strategy. Just made sure everything was okay while moving around in a perfunctory fashion. No one said a word, except Randy Cross,[11] number 51, the intellectual starting guard. This guy never missed a trick. He always gave me the twinkle-in-the-eye kind of look and his broad white smile. Randy was as removed from the stereotypical grunting offensive lineman as the number 4 is to the number 1.

By the way, for Super Bowl champions, their incredibly cramped locker room was tacky and cheesy—like a high school's. Rows of cheap lockers with inexpensive folding chairs of the sort you'd find a church using at its annual bazaar. My locker room was nicer at college during my futile attempt at college ball.

Fun fact: when the players excited, the hallway was so tight, they always departed two players at a time side by side, which turned into a tradition. Montana and Clark, for example, would stroll out together before combining again on third and long in clutch situations.

"What's it like in there?" inevitably someone would ask me from inside our War Room before the games.

"It's mind-blowing seeing the players change at their lockers, converting from citizens of the community by crawling out of a suit and turning into warriors. The final touch is always installing the eye black."

Initially, players applied this black grease under the eyes to reduce the sun's glare. Now they even wore it during night games. It evolved into war paint. Once the eye black goes on, they're ready. Except for those who still had to scream out their traditional primal war cries to their gods.

Each week, I'd walk through the clubhouse before the game acting as if I knew what I was doing. Just a routine. I noted the players used those new Walkmans that recently hit the market, relaxing to handpicked setlists. Slap a cassette tape in, hit play, and *voilà*. What a technology. What will they think of next?

---

11   Randy, a First Team All-American from UCLA, was drafted by SF in the second round in 1976. He enjoyed a thirteen-year career in the NFL and owns three Super Bowl rings. Famous for his mustache, Randy provided constant leadership behind the scenes and in the locker room and was as Niner as anybody else who ever donned the gold helmet.

I checked out Keena Turner and Bill Ring, putting on their oversized pads. Keena was slender and soft-spoken but would be with the Niners through all four of their Super Bowls. So nice and friendly on the outside, but few knew him. He told me stories about growing up in the middle of gang wars in Chicago's gritty Southside. Those Southside suburbs, he said, were war zones. Every morning you wake up and ask yourself if this was the day you leave the planet. The toughness of playing football paled in comparison to danger of that magnitude. A sure tackler, Keena was as tough as a boiled squirrel.

The diminutive Bill Ring was the starting fullback? What was he? Five ten, 190 pounds? How the heck these two guys survived the brutal NFL was beyond me. You think linebacker, you think Dick Butkus, Ray Nitschke, San Huff, or Matt Millen out of Penn State. You think fullback, you think bruisers like Jim Brown, Jim Taylor, Larry Csonka, or Franco Harris out of Penn State. However, Coach Walsh found ways to use the Keena Turners and the Bill Rings and capitalize on their strengths. Not many linebackers covered speedy receivers like Keena. Not many fullbacks ran passing patterns à la wee Bill Ring. They looked and played *huge* on the field.

On the other side of the coin, I checked out Mr. All-Everything, Ronnie Lott, peeling off his street clothes. Nineteen eighty-one's Rookie of the Year and number 1 draft choice out of USC, Ronnie's body looked as if Michelangelo *sculpted* it himself—just perfect, chiseled. He'd go on to become an eight-time First-Team All-Pro Bowl recipient and go down as one of the fiercest hitters and pass interceptors of all time. You knew he was bound to be a future Hall of Famer even back then. Ronnie, the defensive leader, had his game face on, ready to go.

He looked through me. I looked on top of the lockers and kept turning my head. Just doing my job. Everything seemed to be okay, but I could never be sure. Thank God no one's asked me what I was looking for. I never did come up with a good answer.

I checked out the monsters, like the new addition, left tackle Bubba Paris. How entertaining was it watching this six-foot-six, 300-pound-plus-plus-plus gentleman chow down? They ought to charge admission to watch. People would line up. Most people have no inkling how much an NFL lineman ate. It's be*yond* incredible. Four or five thick porterhouse steaks stacked on the plate like pancakes, three baked potatoes, entire bowls of rice, enough colossal portions of veggies and fruit that would feed an entire Vietnamese village. All washed down with quart after quart of milk, 5,000 calories per meal. With all the exercise they got, these "big uglies" had to be careful not to lose any girth. After all, they got paid extraordinary money to get in people's way and transform into immovable objects. Who could move Bubba Paris? No one. You must go around him.

The '83 Forty-Niners proved the Super Bowl rings the '81 Niners wore were no flukes. They battled the powerhouse, defending Super Bowl champion Washington Redskins down to the wire in the NFC Championship game. The game would forever be known as the Forgotten Classic. It was voted one of the best playoff games ever in every poll I've seen. The 49ers lost 24–21 on a late Redskin field goal because the refs blew two calls at the very end of the game:

1. A phantom holding call against Eric Wright. Joe Theismann, the 'Skins QB, threw a desperate long bomb from the Forty-Niner forty-five-yard line that was uncatchable. The rule clearly states it therefore, should be ruled an incompletion. That blown call gave the 'Skins the ball on the Niner eighteen-yard line. The always-quotable Bill Walsh after the game said, "That pass could not have been caught by a ten-foot Boston Celtic."
2. Next, on third and two from the 49er thirteen-yard line, the refs called Ronnie Lott for holding *even though he was nowhere near the incompletion*. He was on the other side of the field. Ridiculous. Fans said, "The fix was in."

Since the game was in RFK in D.C., I wasn't there. They have their own home-field security—why I like Super Bowls, which are at neutral sites, so they needed us.

I heard the locker room afterward was intense. To a man, the 49ers felt they got ripped off. Nothing was more uncomfortable than hearing about some football great crying his eyes out. A team leader,

Dwight Hicks, made a passionate speech. He implored his teammates to remember this feeling, memorize it all offseason, and carry it into next year.

The silver lining in this loss to the 16–2 Redskins: next year, the San Francisco Forty-Niners would have plenty of incentive and motivation after the refs gypped them out of the championship game. Furthermore, everyone circled September 10, 1984, on their calendars. That was when these same Washington Redskins would come to the country's first concrete reinforced park, Candlestick Park, for *Monday Night Football.* But this time, the Niners would enjoy home-field advantage.

And this time, once again, my secret special assignment superseded all others for one reason. It involved . . . girls.

CHAPTER 13

'84: GIRLS JUST WANT TO HAVE FUN

IN '84 MY job evolved even further. Of course, I would never give up my security responsibility inside the locker room before and after games. No way. But I did inherit even more amazing assignments. Real inside stuff called personal guarding.

Each game, El Capitán assigned me to a visiting celebrity. Such was the case on September 9, 1984, *Monday Night Football*, a national holiday in those days—always the number 1 top-rated show each week. Always a sellout. That night, the rock star traveling carnival featuring TV hosts Frank Gifford, Dandy Don Meredith, and O. J. Simpson came to San Francisco. The controversial Howard Cosell had retired the year before.

The defending Super Bowl champion Washington Redskins barged into town as if they owned the place. Niner Nation whispered the word *revenge* throughout the week.

My favorite fascist, El Capitán, commanded in his grating voice, "Your job tonight: make sure 'Skins quarterback Joe Theisman's wife—Cathy Lee Crosby—gets the personal guard. She gets whatever she needs. Remember, she's a celebrity in her *own* right." He pierced the air with his bony digit, aiming it at my eye. "Got it?"

"Sir, yes, sir," I replied, clicking my heels loudly, extending arm and hand, flashing the Roman salute—which he always ignored.

Soon the Niners exited past the red beat-up locker room door and took the field. I put my little stool away and bolted toward my assignment.

Cathy Lee, so very feminine, took my arm lightly and gracefully. We walked incredibly slowly because she decided to wear high heels to the football game. Her hair was unimaginably *big*.

"Congratulations starring in your current smash TV hit *That's Incredible*." I did my homework.

"Oh, you're welcome," she replied in an attractive voice. Her portrayal as Wonder Woman came a year before Linda Carter made the role famous. I also culled a few stories out of her from when she was a professional tennis player performing at Wimbledon on two separate occasions.

We entered the luxury box. Well, luxury by Candlestick measurements. Nothing at all like the new stadiums. Very old looking, dark, and rusty. The bird's-eye view overlooking the forty-five yard line was certainly a different perspective and not bad as far as watching the passing patterns develop. But you didn't feel the hits, hear the bones breaking, or hear the collective thuds after they snapped the ball like down on the field.

The hostess pressed Champagne into Cathy Lee's dainty hand the moment she arrived. I sat in the back watching the game on TV and smirked. I'd *so* rather be on the field in my usual spot. Why go to a game and watch it on TV? Plus, all these stars and VIPs busy yakking it up were not even watching the game until someone scored. Then they would all cheer, hug, and dive back into conversational mode. Plastic.

Inside our box, the roar of the game was muffled. Our hostess was an elderly little lady who once served as a USO entertainer. When she presented me a giant plate of endless food items, my energy level perked up: prime rib, rack of lamb, shrimp, prosciutto, and melon all called to me. I sat ready to wolf it all down when Cathy suddenly cooed, "I'm ready."

How do you spell torture? I took one last longing look at my plate and what could have been. With a tear in my eye and the other on Cathy Lee, off we went to visit celebs in other boxes. This should prove to be a remarkable day—I only wish I weren't starving.

We ventured out into the corridor. Ancient Candlestick did not have the private walkways of other coliseums. Here, I had to make sure the steerage did not hassle my assigned pin-up girl while we bounced from one luxury suite to the next to the next.

She was missing a lot of a game raging below us. I was not too keen on this particular part of this particular job. I brushed aside the riff-raff crowding closer as they recognized my queen, especially those wanting to badmouth all things Redskin. That happened way too much.

"How dare she marry the rival quarterback?" they asked. "What was she thinking?"

Some chucklehead got right in her face. "Cathy, Cathy, please sign this for my daughter. She's a huge fan. Huge!"

Again, unfortunately, my pet peeve entered my mind: El Capitán promotes me but never gives me what I needed most—access to Taser technology.

One drunk after another got in her grill. "Your husband, Theisman, sucks."

See my point? Would have been a helluva lot easier to escort her around these corridors with my Taser.

As we politely sidestepped the drunk, I daydreamed of how nice it all should have been:

"C'mere, derelict. Please allow me to emit a sophisticated pulse wave that utilizes a leading-edge high voltage to penetrate the barriers of the clothing surrounding your body, followed by a lower-voltage stimulation pulse to cause neuromuscular incapacitation." See, I would have been polite about it.

While escorting Cathy Lee to owner Eddie DeBartolo Jr.'s suite, instead of "Please step aside, sir. Let the lady pass," it'd be *zap* goes the Taser. Then I'd pull the trigger three times, running the electrical current throughout the guy's body, overloading his nervous system while creating electro-muscular disruption as he gyrated around like a sick monkey on a stick on the Stick's sticky concrete floor. He'd be flapping like a fish on the sand, terminating in a full fetal position. Then we would nicely step around him.

I must discuss this with El Capitán at our very next meeting. Anyway, we strolled straight into Mr. DeBartolo's suite. She was entertained, but not by Eddie D. He was locked onto the game below, watching his team win a high-scoring nail-biter 37–31, extracting their revenge and letting the league know the Niners were back and determined for more.

Cathy Lee was far from my only plumb assignment. I'll share one more and move on. But how to pick just one? It's impossible. Joe Namath was awesome. A true one of a kind. He may have been known as Broadway Joe, starring in motion pictures and commercials, posing in magazines, and doing ads in Times Square under the bright lights. But I found Joe to be a guy's guy. He'd get in line to order a hot dog and a Coke for the walk. Other celebs would ask me to get them something. And he knew the game's most intricate strategies, telling me what the adjustments would be for both teams in the second half and damn if he wasn't right on the money. Of course, the ladies flocked to him like positive charges to a magnet, and no, I did not even *think* about using Taser technology on the ladies. Well, maybe the ones invading the men's room—no, no, not even them. Gentlemen don't Taser ladies. It's an unwritten rule.

The Niner's fiercest rival, the LA Rams, when in town brought A-list celebrities who flooded our booths, starting with Queen Celeb, Madam Ram herself, the charismatic Georgia Frontiere. Guarding her brassiness was delightful and an honor as she proved a woman could run an NFL team in a male-dominated organization as well as any man. She scooted through seven husbands in all, but it was the death of hubby number 6, Carroll Rosenbloom, that yielded her 70 percent of the LA Rams. Many were surprised the inheritance did not go to Carroll's son, Steve, who was the VP. Georgia fired Steve in four months, taking even more control of the team. Such shrewdness.

Burt Reynolds was a megastar at the time, had two successful football movies on his resume—*The Longest Yard* and *Semi-Tough*—played halfback at Florida State University, and told me turning down the role of Hans Solo in the *Star Wars* enterprise may not have been one of his better decisions. Very down-to-earth fella.

I told Burt that's okay. After all, he still had in his filmography *Deliverance*. When I told Burt that flick was in my top five movies of all time, as well as most of my friends, he flashed one of the brightest smiles you'd ever see. However, I noted the smile quickly vanished when anyone brought up the topic of his wife and his true soul mate, Sally Field. They loved each other, starred in four successful movies together—which Burt would discuss—but any mentioning of Sally Field was verboten as they were breaking up their marriage while being madly in love with each other. Weird, right? Yet so Hollywood.

But let's go with this assignment because it's personal: Each game the opposing team's players provided game tickets for their posses, often called harems or even stables. They would then face this inevitable problem: what to do with their extra ladies after the game? The gals lined up at good ol' Gate A where the action was, where star players like Dwight Clark came out, and where the fans waited for their favorite NFL players who were like rock stars in their eyes. Some of the most beautiful women I have ever laid eyes upon floated around at Gate A. Some classy, some brassy, some good ol' American girls that just wanna have fun.

The country club of the player's mind was always open. Many of the married players flew straight home after the game, not eager to be among the NFL's 80 percent divorce rate.[12]

The single guys, and yes, the married ones, would go, well, anywhere they damn well pleased. Many had practiced abstinence all week to be supremely prepared for the big game. This most likely started in boxing decades ago, and these were the players with a definite mean edge to them. But when the game on the field ended, their little games of sacrifice would abruptly end as well. The fans at Gate A understood the fruits from the player's hard work hung close to the ground, both easily reachable and ready to peel.

Often the player headed back into the locker room for a postgame meeting, especially after a loss. And losing to the Niners in the eighties happened quite often. Some players overextended themselves burning the romantic candle on both ends. In other cities, no problem. The players handed the gals cash who then simply went out on the town and met up with them afterward. However, this act of kindness was rare here

---

12   Greg Bishop, "Taking Vows in a League Blindsided by Divorce," *The New York* Times, August 8, 2009, page 1.

because the city of San Francisco—where the ultimate postgame action awaited—assuming you had a car, was a good forty-five-minute ride with the usual postgame traffic heading north on highly congested 101. Candlestick Park interestingly was not near the city of San Francisco.

One night, the gigantic Washington Redskin tackle Dave Butz, listed as 6'8", 325 pounds, with many reports and opposing players insisting he was even bigger, called me over. Butz was one of the famous Hogs, the legendary massive linemen of the Redskins in those days. They famously weighed his head once and concluded it weighed well over forty pounds. We're talking about a big guy.

Now, to be fair, a lot of times, these players—the 20 percent who remained happily married—nipped temptation in the bud like Dave Butz.[13] But even the devoted men like Dave could become saddled with good female friends expecting to hang out with them. Such was the case that particular evening.

Dave called me over to the actual Gate A. After my hand disappeared inside his, making this my most awkward handshake of all time, he said, "Hey, meet my friend Jody. She flew in from Colorado. She's paranoid about going out into this damn dark parking lot."

There were no lights at the area called Gate A, only dancing shadows flickering within the pitch-dark night. As a rookie guard, I had to be on top of the person to see if it was a fan seeking an autograph, one of the many beautiful women with their agendas, or one of my comrades. But over time, I developed a keen night vision to survey this mysterious, extremely surreal postgame Gate A scene.

A light, cool wind rustled off the bay. His enormous head swiveled around. Judging by his stiff grimace, he, like many before and after, was stunned by the complete total darkness highlighted only by the waning gibbous moon. It hung in the sky like a mysterious amulet around an evil sorcerer's neck. After a game at the Stick, other than the dispersing fans, nothing remained but total darkness and Mr. Moonlight glimmering

---

13   Dave would become the oldest player in the NFL. He was quoted, "Being the oldest player, I have the oldest wife and the oldest kid in the NFL." This set him apart from unmarried or childless teammates. (Bill Lauss, "Grand Old Men Are Bucking the Trend," Pro Sports, *Chicago Tribune* March 12, 1989, section 3 page 13.)

above a macadam parking lot that jutted out into the watery black bay that disappeared into the night and resembled the end of the earth.

Dave peered into the deep night and finally said, "Some fan keeps heckling her out there somewhere."

I looked at the smiling Jody. The heckling was, most likely, because of her jaw-dropping Amazonian figure. Jody Bierwirth prominently stood out like a 3D image in front of a flat crowd shot. Dave's friend and fan, this beautiful buxom blonde would be a perfect match for the giant Mr. Butz if he were available, which he was not.

Suddenly Dave said, "Lissen, you gotta help me out. Show Jody around. I never realized this dump was so isolated. Show her a good time. I got pretty beat up in the game—tell her—and hafta see the trainer."

"But then she's expecting you later, Dave. She might even decide to wait in the lounge until you get taped up. Instead, go with this: 'You gotta attend the dreaded postgame meeting after your tough loss. You're unable to go out afterward. Coach Gibbs frowns upon doing the town after a loss. It looks bad, what with the press everywhere these days.'"

He stared down at me for quite a while, obviously blown away as the players always were, especially the Candlestick newbies, when they suddenly knew I knew what they knew.

"Deal."

He shoved a random wad of cash into my hand, "Promise me you'll spend it."

This cash-wad handoff was quite common and every time was like winning the lottery. I never knew how much would be in these crumpled-up NFL wads, ranging from twenties to hundred-dollar bills. It was always too much 100 percent of the time, but you could never give it back any of it.

I said, "Relax, Dave. I got this. Just give me a minute to change my clothes. I'll take care of everything—this is what I do. I'm a pro at this. I'll show her a fantastic time."

Dave nodded and let out a gust of air strong enough to create waves on the bay water. This *had* become my part-time job within my part-time job, except it paid better than my *still* seven bucks an hour.

"Spend as much of it as you can," he said. Then the giant Dave Butz[14] disappeared, heading back toward the Stick with his body somehow carrying that gargantuan cranium, then he faded away, slipping into a black hole of space that sucked everything into nothingness until . . . gone.

I hopped over to Jody, grabbed her arm, and said, "Let's go. I'm pinch-hitting for Dave. I'll show you a nice night on the town."

If Jody was disappointed, she sure didn't show it. The darkness of night provided perfect cover for the change of clothes folded neatly in the trunk of my sports car. I put on a light blue Oxford shirt, a clean pair of pressed jeans, a tan linen sports coat. I sat on the edge of my trunk, pulled off the black wingtips, and pulled on a pair of sensible shoes. Next, I put the roof back. We hopped over the side and into the copper-colored Fiat Spyder convertible. First car I had ever bought new off the dealership's lot.

Shifting into first, I sped off with Jody. And wouldn't you know it? Prophetically, the first song on the radio was the new Cindy Lauper smash hit. "Girls just wanna have fu-un." That's all they really want / O-o Girls just wanna have fun," we sang along and not necessarily in tune. The climate was warm, lovely, and suddenly most inviting.

These were usually great one-night affairs because the next day, they'd fly off to who knows where. Somewhere *new* like *New* Orleans, *New* York or *New* Jersey. A security guard didn't carry a lot of *cachet*. But this particular assignment turned out differently.

Jody and I hit it off, taking in my favorite haunts and sharing laughs. She never whined even once when her football star failed to emerge. All night long, we did Champagne toasts saying, "To Dave" and dutifully burned through his endless wad of cash.

---

14   Dave played fourteen seasons with the Redskins, sixteen seasons in all, and collected three Super Bowl rings. Ironically, he was a two-time All-Scholastic at his high school Maine South in Park Ridge, IL. Same high school my son Ricky graduated from as well as Hilary Clinton. Small world. Dave starred for three years playing collegiate ball at Purdue University where he made the Collegiate Hall of Fame.

In the wee, little hours of the morning, in the back seat of our stretch limo, she picked up a bottle of Champagne from the car's stock, poured me yet another glass, and asked, "Can you take me somewhere where's there's dancing please?"

"You bet." I hit the button. The little door between the driver and us slid down. I crawled up front and, through the open door, told the uniformed chauffeur, "Starlight Room please, Sir Francis Drake Hotel." You have to be born in Nanticoke, Pennsylvania, deep in the Appalachian Mountains to appreciate moments like this.

Once there, we danced until they closed. Then, arm in arm, we sauntered down the street, Jody as tall as I at six-foot even. We secured a suite on the tippy top of the St. Francis Hotel on Union Square. I lavishly tipped anyone within our proximity. "Which way to the washroom, ma'am? Turn Left? Why, thank you. Here's a Jackson." Even still, my promise to Dave about spending it all proved challenging.

Basking in the morning sunlight permeating our suite, still in good moods, wearing matching white robes and white fuzzy slippers, we shook hands over a mimosa-themed breakfast in bed. We agreed to create a nice little long-distance relationship. Then we made sweet love again.

Jody, like me, an avid skier, and I met for the next several Thanksgiving breaks and a few ski trips in between. We skied like wild banshees and spent quality time together. Just what the doctor ordered for my now two-year-old busted heart. We holed up for a week at a time in Lion's Head Ski Resort in Vail, Colorado, a superb lodge. You can hop on the gondola from the deck right outside your room. The lodge had *the* best heated pool on the planet, both *inside and outside*, for after-skiing relaxation.

We would swim indoors, hold our breath, then swim through a flap through a wall. Once we submerged and surfaced at the other end, we suddenly found ourselves outdoors in the same heated pool, our breath ripped from our lungs as we found ourselves gazing in wonder at the surrounding majestic snow-covered Rocky Mountains or, when at night, up at the brilliant Milky Way.

When the Niners hit the road, I'd sometimes fly in, and we'd take in a Denver Broncos game. Denver also had crazy, dedicated football fans. But mainly, it was always with the skiing. Neither of us ever mentioned the R-word, either. And she never needed to know I was still hung up on JT, two years after the fact. I know, pathetic.

Jody was phenomenal. But long-distance relationships? After a while? *Meh.*

I had a lunch meeting set up with JT to obtain her signatures removing her name from the second deed of trust on the house we bought together and I recently paid off. My plan? I would finally convince her that her new guy was a mistake, a rebound, and what we had was real. Real love. If we could just go out on one innocent date. What harm would there be in that? Then, I'd win her back. Would this plan work? Maybe, but it could be intense.

I met her at the designated restaurant.

CHAPTER 14

'84: HAI BELLE GAMBE

M Y MEETING WITH Joanne had gotten off to a bad start. She sat stoically, arms crossed, and she wasn't very nice. Not at all how I had expected this to fly.

"It's not like you're married yet. Look, how about you and me go out on a simple date, where we won't have all this paperwork between us?" I quickly shoved the now-signed docs into my tan leather briefcase under the table to get the business out of the way. "We can talk about old times, like Hawaii, our cross-country trip or Dakota, our little puppy." I smiled and looked up at her. Will she go for this?

She didn't say anything, just glared. However, her look was pure devastation, as cold as Dracula's grave. Instead, she said, "Why don't you just get a new napkin?"

I never saw this mean side to her. I knew on rare occasions she had a hard side but never vile like this. It caught me totally off guard. I expected her usual sweet self. I looked at the crumpled-up napkin I used throughout lunch. I had shriveled it up into a greasy ball, clutching it and now felt embarrassed, exposed.

"You and me, Joanne, we always got along fine. Remember how we drove cross-country? All those little towns we explored? The perfect summer we called it. We started off with only that one piece of furniture in our new apartment? That big ol' oversized orange couch?"

Damn, thought for sure that'd put a smile onto that face with the determined, straight line for a mouth. "Our vacation in Hawaii? Lying under the stars, listening to the surf and sipping on Primos? Da kine?" Then I moved in for the kill and whispered, "You remember the time at Penn State we skipped our classes and did a picnic out at Whipple Dam? We made love on that huge blanket under the sun. The field sparkled with spring flowers. You laughed your ass off when I went chasing that butterfly au naturel for you, running around that field, remember? Afterward, we lay side by side in love, and then the promises we made?"

"I remember," she said softly, forcing a wry smile.

I reached across the table, taking her hands into mine. I looked at her hand. She still had the missing tan where my ring once lived. I rubbed that sacred spot, her hands full of softness. I looked up, deep then deeper into her emerald-green eyes, highlighted under the dark brown eyebrows below the honey-colored hair. Beautiful. Her expression. What was it exactly? Amore? It looked like, like . . . like . . . like she just drank an entire cup of vinegar. Her eyes suddenly resembled the black eyes of a shark with no soul, swimming in for the kill.

She yanked her hands back then stood and shoved something across the table. "You can have your diamond ring back. It's over between us. Sooner you accept it, the better."

Woman was meaner than a two-headed rattlesnake. Next thing I remember I was sitting at the Holding Company, a bar in the Embarcadero where I knew the bartender, Petey, well and drank myself into oblivion.

The next day could not possibly have come soon enough. Sunday, I escaped my gloom and crawled inside the Niners' locker room earlier than usual. I stood facing the wall, singing to myself as I always do the Beatles', "Here I stand, head in hand, turn my face to the wall."

I slouched onto my stool, replaying yesterday's conversation with Joanne as the players got ready. After such a positive experience with Jody, I went into that meeting *way* overconfident. Bad strategy. Unprepared.

It was 1984, so I just read *1984*. George Orwell talked about the concept of doublethink, the act of simultaneously accepting two mutually contradictory beliefs as correct. I will always love her on one hand and feel we were meant for one another, but on the other hand, I finally realized it was not to be. I had the talk. It went nowhere. Let that one slip right through my fingers. Let it be.

As supreme protector of the door watching the Niners preparing for the battle, I was not my usual high-energy self. No, today I was pretty kicked back. The fact that that damn bartender, Petey, overserved me last night didn't help. My mouth felt stuffed with cotton balls. Everything looked and felt hazy. Thank God for my Forty-Niner distraction.

I sat up, and though I had the blues, I heartily laughed looking around the locker room. The superstitions these guys went through before every game. Unreal. NFL players are the most superstitious creatures on earth. I'm not kidding. I remember thinking I would write them all down in a book someday.

Bill Ring always had to wash his hair with a big ol' bar of Ivory soap. Defensive Coordinator George Seifert[15] would never walk on the 49ers' forty-nine-yard line. He would walk all the way around the 49er helmet logo in midfield as well, never step on it.

He was superstitious about the 49 number especially since the 49ers won the Super Bowl in '89 on his forty-ninth birthday. Before games, he lodged into his other tradition/superstition: taking a shirtless lap around the locker room for good luck. Everyone cheered.

This was a tight team. And I do mean *tight*. Tight as a snare drum. Coach Seifert also wore his lucky blue sweater every single Monday. Eddie D would come down and knock on wood. Ronnie Lott wore his lucky pink plaid shorts before the big games; Dwaine Board just had to have that hot dog at his locker and his shirt turned inside out. "Gotta have my dog," he'd have to say as per the superstition.

This guy always had to eat chicken, and *that* guy always wore his lucky jock strap if he played well the previous week, and *this* guy had to run out onto the field and touch each yard line. Once he went out too early—the forty-yard line was not yet completed—so he returned all the way back into the locker room to wait. Another coach had to be the last man out of the tunnel. Joe Montana, always the happy prankster who

---

15   A Stanford guy and native San Franciscan, Coach Seifert was part of the 49er tapestry like no other. Born in San Francisco, Coach S. ushered Niner home games at venerable Kezar Stadium. He joined the team at the same time as Coach Bill Walsh and would eventually run the defense. His defenses were remarkable. He led the league in fewest points allowed six out of the six seasons. Seifert further served as assistant head coach. After replacing his mentor, Coach Walsh, he won Super Bowls in '89 and '94 and owns five Super Bowl Rings.

had mastered the art of teasing, would tell the coach after he came out that he had to go back to the men's room. Accordingly, the poor coach had to do a 180 and wait in the tunnel while Joe took a whiz.

My all-time favorite superstition bar none: the legendary regimen of the greatest wide receiver in history, Jerry Rice. Nicknamed Fifi— I think that's public knowledge—and they only called him this inside the locker room, mind you. It was because of his poodlelike hairstyle. Anyway, they teased young Jerry for not only his doo but also because of his anal-retention to detail when preparing for each game.

First, Fifi would inspect his body, right down to his perfect fingernails. Next, he would lay out his uniform and clothing he'd soon don for the game in an immaculate manner, all neatly in a vertical row. Then he would inspect each garment and accessory for perfection. Then he would lay out the undergarments, the socks, the T-shirt, then the jersey, the pads—the whole enchilada laid out—in a neat row extending out from the front of his pristine locker. Who could take their eyes off this activity? He'd finally be taping his wrist, and the tape would break—*snap*! *Boom.* That was it. A groan would erupt from his locker neighbors. Off would come every bit of clothing, and Fifi would start his meticulous process all over again.

As the players ran onto the field, I popped a couple of aspirins. Man, I had the mother of all hangovers. I headed down to my old spot on the field, which by now was as comfortable as an old T-shirt. No celebrity guarding assignments today, thank God.

There was comedian Bob Sarlatte, busy cracking everyone up. Madonna was playing through the PA system, so Bob said, "Madonna singing about being 'Like a Virgin' is like the Pope singing 'Just a Gigolo.'"

We all laughed. Bob's comedy was often about current events. He continued, "People should've known about these stories about baseball players doing drugs. The evidence was everywhere. I turned over a baseball card once. You know on the back where it shows career highlights? This card said, 'Steve hasn't slept since 1977.'"

We all buckled over in laughter. Maybe you had to be there, the way Bob delivered the punch lines, but Sarlatte killed. His routine ended when a staff member handed the Voice of the 49ers a laminated card showing today's starting lineups, which he would professionally announce. Bob was the best and even better in the comedy clubs.

Then R. C. Owens dropped his massive hand on my shoulder. The former 49er great asked, "How you likin' bein' a lieutenant now anyways?

"Love it, R. C. It gives me leeway to roam around freely throughout the Stick. El Capitán said, 'Keep an eye out over the entire security operation.'"

"You must be doin' a damn good job."

"That's just it. Not really. I jus' keep showin' up. Four years in a part-time job like this gives you a ton of seniority because turnover's so high—especially after that nasty-ass strike season. Plus, guys ranked ahead of me found it impossible to attend so many Sundays in the fall. They either resigned or miss a ton of games. I miss none. Now, I grab all the cake assignments. Ha-ha."

Which suddenly reminded me, I knew *just* the place to forget about yesterday's lunch fiasco, where my concrete plans crashed like an airplane flying into a mountainside and my heart exploded into fragments. Last year, the powers that be, finally created a top-notch cheerleader program: The Gold Rush. After the annual tryouts, the crème de la crème now led cheers along the sidelines. I figured I had better help guard the twelve cheerleaders running through their pregame performances. Heaven knows they needed some guarding, right?

I made this a routine during the magical '84 season. Eventually, I got to know the Gold Rush quite well. Yeah, I know. It sounds superficial and shallow, hanging with the cheerleaders, but I was light-years beyond caring about anything anymore. And if I may be brutally honest, I am superficial and must confess I was a leg man, and the Gold Rush had the nicest stems on the planet.

One cheerleader, Patti Carson, a Texan, signed my 1984 Gold Rush poster and wrote a personal letter to "little ol' me," as she put it simply because I escorted her dad down onto the field to videotape their routine. She was so thrilled. That favor took me all of forty-five seconds to do. Patti hailed from a small rural southern town, and running cheers in front of 69,732 fans each home game and traveling to NFL cities across the land was her proverbial dream come true. So nice to see.

Patty reached her goal. For others, cheerleading was a stepping stone for a BBD (bigger better deal). I still recall my conversations with one other: this charming, cherubic, cheerful, cheeky cheerleader Teri Hatcher who hailed from nearby Palo Alto. She loved life. Teri worked the Forty-Niner Faithful into such a frenzy, the fans foamed at the mouth. Few led cheers as enthusiastically. Consistently in an upbeat, positive mood, she shared her dreams with me and sincerely believed in them. Then one day, her knight in shining armor arrived. She was *discovered*.

Years later, through hard, grueling work, Teri evolved into a bona fide star of the silver screen, the official *Bond* girl in *Tomorrow Never Dies*, starring across Pierce Brosnan; Lois Lane in *Lois and Clark*; and finally, her apogee, her ongoing role as Susan Meyers in the smash-hit television series *Desperate Housewives*. That role garnered her the Golden Globes Award for Best Actress.

You'd have to say she accomplished her dream rather nicely. It could not have happened to a nicer person than this genuine Niner cheerleader. Positive people like Teri got me through a pretty negative period in my life as did the excitement of the upcoming NFC championship game.

CHAPTER 15

JANUARY 6, 1985: THE NFC CHAMPIONSHIP GAME

S UNDAY SUDDENLY SAW me sitting with Gunner and Brad in the windowless lounge a.k.a. the War Room, the bile-colored walls screaming for a fresh coat of paint. I wrinkled my nose. The place would smell even more like fresh Parmesan cheese this morning if not for that distinct burnt coffee smell overriding everything. Sports sections and magazines, as usual, buried the coffee table. They were shoved aside as Tall Brad arose, walked to the counter, and poured himself a cup of the pungent black grunge. "Want a cup while I'm up?"

I shuddered. "You kidding? I actually value my stomach lining."

Gunner read the *Sporting Green* aloud in his high-pitched voice interrupted by the sunflower seeds going in and out of his pie hole, many clinging to his lower lip. "The Golden State's hot, so the time is right for the best season in Niner history. Keep in mind, the 49ers have been around since 1946, so this 1984 season was magical."

"That writer may be right, but hey, we lose this playoff game in about"—Brad looked at his Mickey Mouse watch—"three hours, then it's all for naught."

The 49ers went 15–1 in 1984. Ray Wersching barely missed a game-tying field goal against the Steelers in the final seconds for their only loss.

"Otherwise they'd've been undefeated," Gunner continued. "They set records for most wins in a season, most road wins going 8–0, in a season and the only time in history an entire defensive backfield, Ronnie Lott, Eric Wright, Dwight Hicks, and Carlton Williamson was elected to the Pro Bowl."

Tall Brad grabbed a chunk and read, "The offense of Joe Montana, Roger Craig, and Dwight Clark grabbed most of the attention, but it's the league's stingiest defense that made this team one of, if not the best team in NFL history."

Like I could read with these guys reading aloud. I said, "The Big D stepped up last week, man, beating the crap out of the New York Giants 21–10. R. C. told me the press never should've labeled this team as a finesse team. That's why they had a chip on their shoulders all year. That and getting gypped in last year's playoffs. It's why they painted 'warrior' on their spikes. The Niner D led the league in fewest points allowed. And Manischewitz, can they hit! Hey, think about it, friends, we win today, we're going to another Super Bowl."

The three of us bolted upright from our chairs, knocking them over. We locked arms, grabbing each other's shoulders and jumped up and down chanting, "Forty, Forty-Niners, Forty, Forty-Niners," until El Capitán popped his head in, a giant sandworm from *Dune* with his mouth as wide-open.

He ended our intellectual conversation by screaming, "Knock it off, you jackasses! How old are you guys anyway? They're here. Now, get crackin'."

We grinned, standing in our circle. They're here. This was it. Gunner whipped out the flask. We each took a long pull, gasped, nodded, then sprinted to help form the security lines surrounding the visiting team entering our fortress: Candlestick Park.

Downstairs, we watched the parade of the visitors, starting with their jubilant cheerleaders. "What're they called again?" I asked. "I forgot."

Brad, our lady's man, answered, "The Honey Bears. However, I hear the owner, Mrs. McCaskey, hates their guts. She's gonna disband them next year when their contract's up. But look, there he is. The one and only."

I followed Brad's point. "That's him all right. Walter Payton, a.k.a. Sweetness. Looks smaller without his pads. Our D better contain his ass. He set the all-time rushing record this year."

Gunner, our repository of stats, said, "12,400 yards. Do you realize that record stood since 1965 when Jim Brown set it? Nearly twenty years ago? And Brown did it in just nine seasons, but hey, Payton's the greatest in our generation. Unreal, huh? What did you say?"

"I said shut up and look. There's Coach Mike Ditka. He's all pissed off already," I said. "How can you be this fuming-mad so early? He just got here."

Something was going down. Ditka was snapping out to somebody about something. It looked quite entertaining until one of the full-time guards started waving for us to get over there. Would've loved to help out, but I had to dash to my job: guardian of the door inside the locker room.

Inside, it was tense. The NFC Championship. I sat on my little stool head down lest some coach yell, "Hey, what the hell is he doing in here?" But no one ever did. Meaningless games I often sat on the other side of the door, but not the biggies.

Fortunately, Coach Bill Walsh, up at the whiteboard, received a gift from the NFL gods: plenty of fodder and newspaper clippings to fire up his team. He used articles from the Chicagoland Area stating how the mighty '84 Bears were just too harsh for San Francisco. They were a meat-and-potatoes team. San Francisco was a finesse team, more comfortable with white wine and quiche.

Say "finesse team" around a Niner. Go ahead. Then you'd better run. Coach quoted verbatim several of the tough Bears. He said, "When people talk like this, all macho, it's to cover up their deficiencies. And the tough talkers are usually very dumb. You 49ers are smart, you play smart on both sides of the ball. You'll prove it today." I scribbled into my Daytimers journal these comments right after the team took the field for warm-ups. His speech was fantastic.

Walsh often excoriated the opposition precisely like this inside the secret sanctimonious locker room. He was as tough as an old grizzled rodeo-riding cowboy before his players. This was juxtaposed against his image when asked about the opposition in front of the public. He always complimented them to the paparazzi. The nasty-ass side of the former boxer inside the locker room versus the cerebral, always-polite professor on the outside.

The game and the West Coast Offense got underway. People don't understand the West Coast Offense. But was it ever on display this game. Wow. After setting up the short passing game with quick strikes to both receivers and backs like Wendell Tyler, it resorted to a grinding running offense with Roger Craig high-stepping through the line of scrimmage, his knees pumping upward like pistons. Whenever I told the fans that this new offense was 60 percent run, they were blown away. That's the biggest unknown about this offense. Coach also unveiled a new soon-to-become-famous wrinkle to the attack this week.

It was this—surprise! Walsh stuck it to the tougher guys of hard-nosed Mike Ditka. Guy McIntyre, a badass 271-pound offensive guard, smoke pouring out from his nostrils like a cartoon bull dragging his hooves across the ground preparing to charge. He lined up in the backfield on short yardage plays. Walsh pounded him into the Bear's defensive line like a wrecking ball smashing through a brick wall. McIntyre blasted massive holes into the famous Bears defensive line. The Niner backs simply glided through these holes like skaters at Rockefeller Square. Not much finesse there, blowing massive holes in the line, was there? No, sir. The point pounded home as to who was the *mas* macho team. They came from "the City by the Bay, not the City by the Lake. They came from the City that Knows How"[16]—not the Windy City of Wide Shoulders.

The pugilistic Bears got waxed. San Francisco, apparently the more physical team, proved it. They stuck the hallowed doughnut on the Bears side of the scoreboard like a cowboy branding a zero onto his steer's butt, embarrassing the former Monsters of the Midway. They shut Da Bears of Mike Ditka out, 23–0.

Here's me on the right, with a guard on my left, long after the game, the only on-field photo I ever had taken (and yes, I know my clip-on tie doesn't reach the buckle):

---

16   This line was penned by famous *SF Chronicle* writer Herb Caen.

The victory meant it was Super Bowl time again.

Brad, who somehow inside the stadium had gotten stoned already, didn't even know where the big game was and asked me.

"Why you gotta know, Brad? Maybe this time we'll travel to an exotic tropical location instead of freezing our tails off like in Detroit. *Brrr*—bitter memories."

"Just tell me where it's at."

"Guess."

"New Orleans? Miami? San Diego? Gotta be somewhere erotic, right?"

"You mean exotic, Brad, and no, it's not in any one of those cities."

CHAPTER 16

JANUARY 6–12, 1985: THE ADVENTURES OF THE OFFICIAL SUPER BOWL VAN

N OPE . . . Super Bowl XIX week was in our backyard, a mere fifteen-minute commute from Candlestick to where both Bill Walsh and George Seifert coached—Stanford Stadium. Can you believe it? We'll never make it to the promised lands.

It was versus the hottest team in America—the Mighty Miami Dolphins. Dan Marino versus Joe Montana drew all the primary press coverage leading up to the showdown between two western Pennsylvanian quarterbacks of Italian heritage who had both thrown for over 3,000 yards during the season, a Super Bowl first. It would become the largest viewing audience in the history of television sports: the Game of the Century.

Dan Marino, of the *GQ* looks and the golden aura, the 1984 Most Valuable Player, completed the greatest season for a quarterback in NFL history, breaking six single-season passing records. They included most touchdown passes, forty-eight, and most passing yards 5,084, in a single season.[17]

Miami's mighty Marino mastered massive passing attacks that led the Dolphins to a 14–2 regular season record, averaged over four touchdowns per game, and blazed a trail of fire throughout the playoffs, crushing Seattle 31–10 and mutilating the vaunted Pittsburgh Steelers defense in the AFC title game, 45–28. People and paparazzi perpetually

---

17   This Hall of Famer would go on to become one of the greatest NFL quarterbacks in history and was currently fifth all time in victories.

pestered Marino everywhere he went. In this, just his second NFL season, he had attained rock star status.

The three of us waited outside El Capitán's office. This time I knocked louder on his door. With the Super Bowl one week away and us not getting to travel anywhere, his assignments should be interesting.

I said, "The City is animated. San Franciscans were sick to death hearing that their first Super Bowl three years ago was a fluke, an aberration, and an anomaly."

Gunner, chewing, spitting, always in motion, and as usual, smirking, said, "I know. No one can believe how it seems only one team's coming to play—the Miami Dolphins."

Brad added, "Sorry, guys, but Miami's gonna beat San Francisco rather badly because—"

El Capitán, snakelike, had quietly slid out of his office enshrouded inside a cloud of tobacco smoke. He provided his own cover. He heard what Brad said and shot him the look containing two steely knives. He mumbled, "Fuckin' traitor," under his breath. But we heard it. El Capitán called me in. Together we entered the cloud.

But not before I turned to Brad. "Well, you're certainly going to get a plum assignment, idiot."

Brad only smiled and said, "Everyone knows Miami's gonna win."

I entered and sat before the fascist. He had that little power game going, where the chair before his desk was low so you had to look up at him in his way-higher chair as though you were before an Egyptian pharaoh. After he sat behind his power desk, I asked, "How you doing, El Capitán? First Super Bowl ever in the Bay Area, and it's right here, a virtual home game for us. Any thoughts on that?"

My question had nothing to do with his draconian security business laws, so he ignored it. El Capitán despised small talk.

"Your weeklong assignment: driving the official Super Bowl van around the City. You'll be picking up and escorting dignitaries and such, hustling them from the private jet parking lot at SFO to the social events and hotels."

My wiry boss was always the same throughout my years at Burns Security, all business all the time. However, this one time, I think I may have ever-so-slightly caught just the tiniest hint of a twinkle in his eye. He knew I ate this stuff up. He also knew I was in sales and could take a week off.

The official Super Bowl van parked anywhere it damn well pleased. If you ever tried parking in San Francisco, you'd understand why this was a treat. People cheered when the official Super Bowl van pulled up. It took on a life of its own. Everyone got such a kick out of it. I ushered the Gold Rush to a cheerleader party, and the gals decorated the insides using red and gold. Not until hours later did I realize I had perfectly formed kiss marks on my cheeks.

Finally, at long last, no more troubles getting dates, especially to "help me," attend the Super Bowl parties around the vibrant city. The Official Super Bowl Van finally banished Joanne into the deep recesses of my mind.

On January 12, the *San Francisco Chronicle*'s Pink Pages (the entertainment section) listed twenty-eight Super Bowl parties. Perhaps the one and only time I armed myself with the ultimate pickup line at the clubs: "Yeah, sorry, can't stay . . . I got this VIP party to attend. Top of the Mark Hotel, you know, keep an eye on things. Hey, just wondering. If you'd like to hop in the official Super Bowl van parked out front and have a few drinks with some of the NFL owners, players, celebs, that sorta thing . . . Well, you know, I could use a little help entertaining."

At the Mark and during the festivities, I packed the official Super Bowl van with celebrities, sports stars, politicians and had an attractive lady on each arm, diving deep into the superficiality of it all. Me, a loser who previously couldn't even get a gal to return a call.

And I'm not going to get plastic and start dropping names of people I rubbed shoulders with such as Bob Hope, Danny Thomas, Lee Iacocca, Jimmy the Greek, Merlin Olsen, Jim Brown, Burt Reynolds, Herb Caen, and Howard Cosell who rode shotgun, so don't worry about that.

The OSBV (official Super Bowl van) drove Tony Bennett down to city hall where we all caught Tony belting out his legendary, "I Left My Heart in San Francisco." Had to be his best version ever.

The SB Van cruised to the Moscone Center a.k.a. The Official 49er pep Rally, that ran from 7:00 PM until 1:00 AM. I merely held on to the steering wheel. Everyone waved. Cars honked, and thumbs-up signs shot out the car windows at the OSBV crisscrossing the steep hills of the City. The van hopped up on the sidewalk right in front. As security gushed out, I merely flashed my creds and exclaimed, "This is the official Super Bowl van."

"Of course," said the valet. "Leave it right there, and we'll guard it with our lives." I smiled broadly and ushered my guests inside. This whole scene was too great.

The spirit of San Francisco is extraordinary and just another reason I love this city so. The entire city gets in on concepts such as this. Best example ever was when Emperor Norton patrolled its streets as the golden city's self-proclaimed ruler or, as he put it, "Emperor of the United States and Protector of Mexico."

He reigned from September 17, 1859, and for twenty years afterward. Joshua Norton, though penniless, attained celebrity status, ate for free at local restaurants, and was most welcome by the proprietors. It became apparent that having the emperor inside your establishment meant additional paying patrons would lunch or dine, including tourists. These tourists traveled from afar for a photograph of the Golden Gate Bridge, Lombard Street, a cable car, Coit Tower, and the emperor. The loyal subjects, ranging from Mark Twain to Robert Louis Stevenson, adored Emperor Norton. All bowed or bent the knee whenever in the presence of the mighty emperor.

Another example was the adventures of Batkid. On November 15, 2013, staging the most massive Make-A-Wish project ever, Batkid a.k.a. Miles Scott, had leukemia. But, he made headlines and national television news as he saved the city (in his black Lamborghini disguised as the Batmobile) from evil villains such as the Riddler and the Penguin. He saved a damsel in distress about to be crushed by the nation's only moving national historic monument, the cable car.

Miles's dream, when asked by the foundation, was unique. He wanted to be Batman. On Batkid Day, the foundation sent out a request for volunteers to help with the staging and to wear costumes. They hoped to get a few dozen people but worried only a dozen or so would show up.

Twelve thousand San Franciscans proudly took the day off from work expecting to be saved by Batkid and turning Batkid Day into an epic event. SF made it come true for Miles Scott by converting the entire city into Gotham City. Thousands of more Americans from nearby towns poured into Gotham City once the word went out on social media. People flew in from other countries. Everyone asked, "How can I help?" People read about it on the front page as an exclusive story in the *San Francisco Chron*. Every former Batman called him. The president of the United States Barack Obama called and personally thanked him for saving Gotham City. Signs everywhere were held proclaiming, "Save us Batkid." And he did—boy did he ever. The world saw what a city could do when motivated by a warm and fuzzy cause.

They even made a tremendous award-winning documentary about it. I challenge you to watch this trailer below and finish it with a dry eye.[18]

Really, take a moment please and put this URL into your browser. Your heart will be rewarded. Thus, in this spirit, the Official Super Bowl van remained in front of the Moscone Center. Inside, I found myself dancing with my two new friends in between the three stages of live acts. This included the middle stage we were at, showcasing the red-hot Pointer Sisters. I didn't bother pinching myself as the Sisters sang their hit "Jump (For My Love)." To say spirits soared high would be an understatement.

The other significant part of this weeklong assignment was going undercover, meaning wearing regular clothing and shedding the hated polyester. Unlike cotton, the synthetic fabric never breathes. Plus, it was uber cool merely flashing my badge whenever needed instead of wearing it.

At sunrise, on Super Bowl Sunday, El Capitán yanked me in. I already knew what to expect. He was going to mention how I'd been showing up at all the extravaganzas, staying late and bringing people along with me as unregistered guests. He will undoubtedly chew me out regarding the unregistered young ladies I brought up onto that rooftop party last night on top of the Stafford Hotel and how their antics contributed to that particular party getting out of control. Yeah, it just plain got wild. I'll counter with "but none of that was my fault, Supreme Commander."

---

18   https://www.youtube.com/watch?v=gxKvVInY8JE

People had to understand the first 49ers Super Bowl caught everyone by surprise. That team was ridiculously young. Montana's first full season at the helm, they started 1–2, and no one in their infinite imaginations gave a modicum of a possibility we'd ever get past Dallas. This time, however, the City by the Bay prepared in earnest even though once again, the smart Vegas money poured in on the fish.

El Capitán pointed his bony finger straight at me as I stood in front of his desk. Here it comes. I bit deeply into my lower lip.

"Pregame assignment: guard Bill Walsh's daughters and nieces, all the way until you work the locker room on game day. You got it?"

"Yes, El Capitán, sir." *That's it?* I thought.

In a voice as dry as an Arizonian sun-drenched gravel road, he added, "Now, after the players leave the locker room, I have your Super Bowl special assignment—let's call it SBSA. I want you to sit down and absorb what I'm about to tell you."

I listened to his rap carefully as he continued sucking in smoke like a vacuum cleaner. After hearing my Super Bowl special assignment, I wondered, did he mix me up with somebody else? Didn't he know who I was? These essential assignments are of considerable gravitas. I'm a terrible guard. There are others way more into this than I.

Meanwhile, escorting these bubbly young Walsh ladies around to the various tailgate parties and meeting their friends and relatives was a blast. I found the Walsh family to be a jovial and tight family. But I still knew my big special SBSA loomed ahead. And when I learned what it was, well, it blew my mind.

CHAPTER 17

SUPER SUNDAY

January 20, 1985
Pregame, Super Bowl XIX

THE PREGAME ANTICIPATION bubbled over like the brew in a cauldron. Smoke from the grills encircled Stanford Stadium in its entirety, the rich scents permeating the walls of old. Colorful balloons and costumes added to the atmosphere. Even the famous SF fog made an appearance, thick, drifting low around the Stanford Stadium, keeping the scene contained, cool, and cloudy. It traveled like smoke on the winds coming off the peninsula's bay. My time with the gregarious Walsh girls was grand and ended too quickly. I hugged them tightly, said goodbye, promised to write and headed for the sanctuary of my tiny stool at the locker room door.

I could not wait to hear Coach address the team. If I had any brains, I'd have been writing down his many gems of wisdom all season long, not just randomly.

Arriving, I saw a crowd had gathered outside the door. ABC had the bright lights going. This was their first Super Bowl, and they were hustling for scoops. Coach Walsh performed a pregame interview. Burns Security guards stationed themselves strategically to keep the press at bay and especially the overzealous ABC in line. I listened in. The reporter, with oily lips and showing off a gathering of adipose between his shirt and pants, asked Coach Walsh, "Why are you the first coach considered as 'the Genius'?"

Coach replied, "I don't know. Maybe it's my gray hair."

Both reporter and the crowd laughed. Reporter said, "I think it's because you never say, 'No comment.' You always come up with some kind of answer."

I turned to Gunner. If his hat were any lower, he wouldn't be able to see. The lad chewed like crazy, standing among the guards keeping an eye on the press. I said, "I think it's because Coach's so cool and calm in theses hairiest of situations."

Gunner thought about my comment and replied, "I think it's 'cos he always had the first thirty plays scripted, choreographed if you may. Thus, he always jumped out to the lead. I heard him once say regarding his preparations, 'Flying by the seat of your pants precedes crashing by the seat of your pants.'"

Suddenly, from above, a familiar voice boomed. Gunner and I looked up. R. C. Owens.

In charge of alumni relations, he was bringing former Niner greats into the locker room to stoke the flames and get the players psyched.

R. C. added, "I think it's 'cos a' how great he recruits. Coach drafted this whole team. No one even knows how he got a Joe Montana or the superb Dwight Clark."[19]

Like it was a secret. After making us practically get down on our knees and beg like peasants in a European village to tell us, jeez. After nodding my head vigorously for him to proceed, he went on—finally.

"Coach sends his quarterback's coach, Sam Wyche, down to UCLA to try out this new kid, a collegiate star named James Owens, see? So you gonna try out a receiver without someone throwin' to him? I don't think so. So, Mr. Walsh, he finds out Mr. Montana jus' a-happens to be in UCLA shackin' up with his girlfriend over in Manhattan Beach.

---

19   Dwight will go down as one of the greatest of all 49ers, and not just for being the other half of the immortal Catch. Not just for his 506 career catches or his 6,750 yards or for his 48 touchdowns, his All-Pro seasons or his two Super Bowl rings—but for the many clutch catches he made in crucial situations. After the Niners retired his number 87, they hired him to be the team executive. Later, Dwight served two years as the Cleveland Browns general manager and director of football operations. Like too many former NFL players, Dwight felt football was the primary reason he passed away from Lou Gehrig's disease.

Coach calls Joe. 'Hey, c'mon over to campus. Throw some balls to Owens as he runs routes.'

"Sam comes back next day. Reports to Coach Walsh about Owens. 'Coach, Owens looked good, but you gots to see this kid throwin' to him. Every pass, spot on—I mean, on the money. I never seen someone throw such a catchable ball.'

"So next thing you know, Coach Walsh, he gives him a look. He loves his footwork, his agility, his precision, and his passing accuracy. He looked for a reason to pass on him. Everyone else did. Coach found no reason. So he nabs him in the third round. Think about that, eighty-one other players got picked before this quarterback well on his way to becomin' the greatest of all time. But only coach knowed it at the tam, you see?

"You ought a seen Joe when he first arrived to camp." R. C. let out a loud guffaw, cracking himself up. "Skinny-ass 185-pound honkey with legs lookin' like they be stickin' out of a bird's nest."

We all cracked up. I barely managed a peek toward the locker room. Still pregame interviews. I had time. So I listened for more of the latest edition of R. C. Owens' inside stuff. This guy had all the good stories.

R. C., big watery eyes sloshing around, went on. "Dwight Clark tol' me, 'First time I met Joe, he was this scrawny kid with a blonde Fu Manchu. I thought he was a Swedish placekicker.'"

Again, we roared with laughter. Does anyone else know all this?

R. C. knew he had us spellbound and was on a roll. "Trust me, son, anyone tellin' you 'cept Coach they thought Joe'd amount to a hill of beans, they be lyin'. Now, he gonna be a legend. 'Specially after today."

Gunner, all excited by the story, whispered, "He's right. Joe's gonna kick ass today. I gotta get to a pay phone. I'm backing up the Brinks Truck on this one. You want in on some action?"

My heart began racing. Should I? "No," I told him. "I feel the Niners'll win, but I hate layin' points."

"You'll be sorry." Gunner split to add to his bet. But I figured he wasn't looking at this game very objectively, so I had no regrets.

The tall Niner ambassador, R. C., broke off and ushered several alumni into the locker room, after saying, "Goodbye," to the ones who left. Former Niner greats kept coming and going to wish the players good luck and share wisdom.

Tall Brad nauseatingly flashed his Micky Mouse watch, gave us the time, and asked, "You think that's a true story? Sounds like a 'Paul Bunyan and the Blue Ox' kinda thing."

"I stood right next to R. C. for several seasons, Brad. He doesn't ever bullshit. Not like you. Look he's free. Grab'm."

Brad did, and I asked, "R. C. you said something about Dwight Clark too."

"Even better story, Rick. Check this out:

"Our brand-spankin' new white-haired coach goes to Clemson, right? Same year, 1979. His first year as coach and he's doin' all his own recruiting, building a team in his vision, see? He's tryin' out the kid from Clemson they wanna draft as the new franchise quarterback, Steve Fuller. Guy's got a gun for an arm, right? He's marked as a number 1 draft pick." R. C. yawned wider than a lion. He yawns even though he's not tired. It's what he does.

He continued, "Well, they need someone to run routes for Fuller, but it's spring break or sumpin'. No one's around. They call Dwight Clark, a guy that hardly ever played on the Clemson team. He sat the bench all season. He would have nothing better goin' on, right? Dwight wasn't even gonna answer the phone 'cos he had his golf bag on his shoulder and was walkin' out his door.

"Opportunity ringed. Dwight takes the call but must decide. Run routes for someone bein' given a look? Nuthin' in it for him. Or golf. He decides hey, if I can get in front of a head coach, do it.

"Clark runs the routes for Fuller. Coach is blown away. But more by Clark than Fuller. Crazy, right? He runs razor-sharp precision routes, great feet, and he dropped this many passes." R. C. forms a zero with his right hand. "He had better hands than me."

The former star receiver of the Niners holds out what had to be the most massive hands I've ever seen. Black as oil on the backs, white as ivory on the palms. And the size? Jesus, you could paint a billboard on them and have him stand on the side of the 101 freeway.

"And quick." He grabs my head with both his hands and gives me a playful shake. You had to love this guy.

R. C. continued, "Kid had hardly any game film on him because he never played. Coach realized no one knows about him, not even his own team so he doesn't draft him until—get this—the tenth round. Dwight Clark will break every franchise receiving record here by the time he's done—mark my words. But Coach, man, I gotta tell ya, he saw somthin' in that kid no one else did."

Fan favorite Dwight Clark did, in fact, go on to break every Niner receiving record when his nine seasons as a 49er concluded. His number 87 was retired by the franchise, and he went down as the franchise's best receiver of all-time sans Jerry Rice. Dwight had 506 catches for 6,750 yards and 48 touchdowns. He led the NFL in receptions during the 1982 season and made the Pro Bowl twice in 1981 and 1982. Of course, his name is synonymous with perhaps the most excellent play in NFL history, the Catch.

Brad and Mickey announced the time. His obsession does come in handy every once in a while. Everyone departed except me. I settled on my little stool inside the main locker room door for my pregame assignment. Great stories. Coach Walsh, such a mind.

This mind displayed itself before the main event in the land of pregame preparations. The first coach ever referred to as the Genius subtly appeared with his anticipated pregame pep talk. However, this particular Super Bowl, he started as strangely as you could imagine.

The tension was as thick as a politician's skull. Miami, many said, was the best team of all time. The smart money was all pouring in on the 'Fins. Even most pundits in the local San Francisco press predicted a Dolphin victory.

The players sat waiting for Coach to take his customary spot up at the whiteboard, where he loved to draw while he spoke. This should be a treat for him, a déjà vu, as he stood at this same board while coaching Stanford.

I made double sure the door closed then sat on my little stool and melted into a landscape as familiar to the players as a window. The scene was surreal and claustrophobic, waiting in this college locker room while millions of eyes around the world waited just beyond walls closing in from the pressure outside. The walls leaked from the intensity of the pressure outside like an old high school boiler in the basement. Hearts were pounding, most everyone sat and stared at the whiteboard, waiting for one white-haired wizard.

Coach was lying down in the back of the room, however. He gave me the *shhh* sign. The 49ers heard their future Hall of Fame coach's voice from the rear. They snapped their collective heads around from facing the whiteboard.

Coach still kicked back on the floor in the locker room. Players not yet seated, heading for their spots, stepped over him. He stretched and yawned, demonstrating how relaxed he was. Arms crossed behind his head, comfortably propped up against a bag of footballs, legs crossed, he casually perused the magazines and newspapers he brought in for some reason. The great motivator next stifled another yawn. The players' faces were dually composed of shock and humor.

The great coach casually launched into a monologue: "I don't know, guys. Maybe we shouldn't even bother going onto that field today. We could just forfeit. We certainly can, you know. After all, this is the Miami Dolphins. Everyone and their brother knows their offense will be marching up and down the field on us all day. Why get embarrassed? I mean, look at Dan Marino on the cover of this magazine."

He held it up for inspection—handsome Dan on the cover throwing a pass to one of his two famous Marks, Mark Duper and Mark Clayton. Then another magazine, then another—even non-sports magazines. All about Dan and the Dolphins.

"He's having the best season a quarterback ever had. In fact"— Coach dug through the large pile looking—"I don't see a single thing about our quarterback. Oh. Wait. Here's one."

He held up the January 21, 1985, *Sports Illustrated* showing both QBs in action, Dan the Man first. I looked and saw Joe Montana's ears getting red. Nobody competes as intensely as Joe in anything.

Coach opened up a newspaper. You could hear a marshmallow land in the room. "You know, I thought we had a decent defense this year." He looked from his paper to his brooding team. "I mean, we gave up the least amount of points in the entire league, right? But just read this article here in our very own newspaper, the *Chron*. This writer predicted, 'a Marino career day and predicted a blowout.' Listen. 'The Niners were too slow and susceptible to Dan's quick release. Look for a Dolphin victory and by a wide margin.'"

I checked out an enraged Ronnie Lott. He shook like a boiling teapot ready about blow its lid.

You get the picture. On and on, Coach rambled in this purely sarcastic vein. He painfully pointed out how literally nothing, absolutely nothing, was said about this remarkable defense. The press across our great land, amazingly including our own, picked the Niners not only to lose but to lose big as well.

"Why even go out there and get pounded, right, guys? Wad'ya say? Let's hang it up. Call it a day. You guys okay with that? Let this one go? Seriously. Let's cash it in. After all, what chance do we have"—he stood; they all stood—"against *the mighty Miami Dolphins, the team of the century*? What do you think guys? Let's give up. Shall we?"

Life contains, from time to time, those special moments compressed like diamonds. Such was the case. Suddenly the ice-cold, piercing blue eyes of Bill Walsh locked onto my blue eyes. I noticed that I, like everyone else, was hyperventilating. Emotions swirled within to the point I felt weird tears forming behind my eyes. Bill Walsh, head coach of the San Francisco Forty-Niners, and Rick Pucci, a former derelict from a backwater coal town called Nanticoke deep in the Wyoming valley inside the Appalachians, stared at each other. The juxtaposition of the top of the food chain, Bill Walsh staring at the bottom, a lowly security guard. Our joint journeys juxtaposed together at this juncture in time. It went unnoticed among the players shouting at each other. Our blue eyes connecting, our lives intertwined with one another, both of us bonded, not only by the fact that we both attended San Jose State University but also by the fact we were staring at each other before the 1985 Super Bowl.

It went eerily quiet. The time had come. All you heard was the muffled murmur of tens of thousands on the other side of the walls. A calm eternity passed. The white head nodded. My forever Forty-Niner moment had arrived. Right on cue, I stood. I did it. I opened the door, performing admirably. I contributed in my humble way to the cause. Okay, anybody could've opened a simple door, but let it be.

The San Francisco Forty-Niners, filled with wrath, in their classic red jerseys and gold pants, became a raging stampede rushing through that door. I dove to the side just in time, getting out of the way of Pamplona's Running of the Bulls; but truth be told, the 49ers didn't need the door. Entirely on fire, they could as easily have run right through the wall, amidst a current of some of the worst cussin' I've ever heard. In fact, the players invented nasty epithets about the Dolphins, showing the same imagination that put Neil Armstrong on the moon. Man, they were PO'd.

I ran outside the stadium to my next juicy assignment, the Super Bowl Special Assignment or SBSA, rubbing my hands together, grinning like a little schoolboy and thinking, *Oh boy, oh boy, this is gonna be good.*

Upon my arrival to my designated spot at the Walsh family's 49er tailgate party, you could tell this tailgater was for the insiders. Not by the fancy spreads of banquet food laid out on red and gold covered tablecloths, mind you. Not by the variety of meats and grilled vegetables. Vegetables? Who grilled vegetables? Not by the smoking prime steaks on the silver-plated grills creating massive silos of smoke billowing up and becoming one with the fog-enshrouded sky. No, not by the lavish consumption on display.

No, it was because of their attire. Most fans wore red-and-gold color schemes or the official 49er jackets. These folks wore formal reds and golds as in gold tweed sports coats, red casual slacks, 49er neckties, spectacular 49er jewelry, and such. Here was red and real gold on display. Here, they introduced me to my gold, my daylong assignment, my SBSA, guarding Bill Walsh. Yes, I would now guard Bill Walsh.

Bill Walsh Senior, that is. Our coach was a junior. Senior traveled via wheelchair and came with a mystery I did not yet know. Also, on hand was Coach Bill Walsh's uncle who introduced us. He bragged how he bet a ton on the 49ers and didn't give a rat's ass how many points he gave. He said we'd win big. Wish I was that confident. He was one of the rare ones.

Initially, I thought Bill Walsh Sr.'s mind was as sharp as a tack, especially when the gruff old man said, "Hurry up and eat. I wanna see who's gonna murder the national anthem this year."

Here is a shot of the venerable Bill Walsh Sr. sporting the one-glove look and Coach Bill Jr.'s uncle donning a red vest and golden sports coat, Super Bowl tailgating:

So, I gulped down some brie, of all things, which I can definitely live without, some succulent grilled prawns or was it jumbo shrimp—can anyone tell the difference? When does a jumbo shrimp become a prawn anyway? They offered caviar, but I said, "No thanks. Saving that for my honeymoon," which of course struck me with a pang of regret over Joanne.

This menu sure differed from the burger-laden tailgates we usually attended. I kept my eye out for that boisterous big bald black dude from the currently popular Miller High Life commercials who takes the Millers back to his truck because we were too uppity and thus unworthy.

I rinsed it all down by draining a glass of ice-cold Anchor Steam. After saying my goodbyes to the entire Walsh family, I pecked the cheeks of the Walsh daughters and nieces I befriended and trully liked. They were too sweet.

I pushed Bill Walsh Sr., nestled under his 49er cap and firmly under his plaid blanket, toward our designated spot. This time I was not going to be on the field. Nevertheless, I screamed once again after the usher gave us our seats.

"What're you yodeling about?" Bill Sr. asked. I could tell right up front he didn't like me.

"I pinched myself. I didn't realize the handicap section sat smack dab on the fifty-yard line."

"Why, where'd you think they'd shove us? In the end zone?"

"Well, no, I, uh, never knew where the disabled sat, but I didn't think you got the best seats in the house. I mean, uh, I'm not saying you don't deserve—"

"Just let it go," he commanded. So gladly, I did.

To think this all started from that simple thought process at the City Tavern, wolfing down breakfast with Van four years ago. Maybe I'm not such an idiot after all. I was getting paid to sit on the fifty-yard line at the Super Bowl with the head coach's father. Maybe there's hope for me after all.

I let out a long chest full of air and looked around the sold-out 84,000-seat Stanford Stadium. "What an amazing year it's been, sir, to be young and dumb in sunny California."

He didn't reply. I glanced over at him.

Ah, look how stiff and quiet Bill Walsh Sr. looked. The poor guy slipped into a daze, his eyes glazed. Just got too old, that's all. Once the game starts, I'll explain the finer intricacies to him about the action. He'll like that. I decided to start a conversation. Otherwise, he'll sit there completely quiet all game. I'm too excited just to sit like a bump on a log.

"Here are a few examples why. Ever hear of the local San Francisco band, Huey Lewis and the News? No? They put out their seven-time-platinum album *Sports* earlier this year with hits like "I want a New

Drug" and "The Heart of Rock 'n'Roll" . . . Is Still Beatin'." I sang this last part, getting psyched, realizing this was a fifty-yard-line seat for the Super Bowl. I continued, "Their music blares over the airwaves all the time, sir. Plus, you should've seen the incredible energy and unbridled success of the amazing spirit of the 1984 Olympic Games. This spirit soared all over Los Angeles, California, like the great white eagle."

"How would you know?"

"I dropped out of corporate America for two years and hired on as a regional director and raised hundreds of thousands in charitable funds for American amateur athletes. Consequently, I was rewarded prime seats to all the main Olympic events."

He remained unimpressed.

"Look, Mr. Walsh, quickly, up on the screen."

The flags of California flew everywhere surrounding the stadium. But we focused on the big screen. To further my point, California's very own governor Ronald Reagan appeared via satellite. Ronnie went all the way and won the presidency. His inauguration occurred earlier today, the same exact day the Super Bowl was hosted right here in California. He flipped the coin toss. How cool was that? Ah, technology. A cheer erupted from the fans. Of course, the 49ers won the toss. The crowd went bananas.

"This is gonna be our day, Mr. Walsh." I was so excited I nearly burst.

Mr. Bill Walsh Sr. and I watched the new soon-to-be-famous Apple ad[20] quietly.

I did not yet know the mystery of Mr. Walsh, but I would learn it soon enough with all its bells and whistles.

---

20   Outside the walls of the Super Bowl in the heart of Silicon Valley, where Stanford sat, the Apple Macintosh computer flew off the shelves for the first time. In fact, Apple won all the awards for their commercials that year with this ground-breaking award-winning TV spot, whose only national showing occurred during the California Super Bowl. Here's the link or just search for 1984 Apple ad: https://www.youtube.com/watch?v=OYecfV3ubP8

CHAPTER 18

THE GAME OF THE CENTURY—NO, REALLY

January 20, 1985
Super Bowl XIX

"WE WON THE toss, Mr. Walsh. Now the world will see your son's amazingly scripted, choreographed plays."

He didn't reply nor say anything to me. He looked out of it, disinterested.

"The press asked Bill outside the lockers about why he's considered a genius." I then proceeded to tell him how the genius motivated the team.

This snapped him back. "Bill's a boxer, not some sissy-ass genius. He boxed at college."

"He did? Wow, no one knows that. Ha. Once again, like the prankster Montana, or the studious Hacksaw Reynolds, the perception did not match the persona."

"You could fill three books with what you don't know," the older Walsh lectured. "He was a damn good boxer too. Won plenty of fights. That's how I raised him. He knows how to counterpunch and how to size up the competition. He'll beat you to the punch every time. And he knows the importance of getting into the rhythm. That's how he coaches and motivates."

The game abruptly ended our conversation. I marveled as I gazed at the field.

These perfect fifty-yard line seats in the mezzanine level were unreal. One of my pet peeves was hearing the bragging of the couch potato bray, "I got the best seat in the house. Right here in front of the TV."

No, Mr. Potato Head, you don't. First off, you don't get to see the San Francisco Gold Rush right up front like this celebrating the game's first score. I snapped a photo using an everyday Nikon 35-mm camera with no zoom lens. That's my photo, and there is Teri Hatcher, first row, extreme left. The squad's captain was to her immediate right. They had the hometown crowd fired up.

There's also the obvious about live games being better than big screen versions: not being able to replicate the sights, smells, and spontaneity of being in the big crowd. On TV, all you saw was the quarterback taking the snap, handing it off or throwing a pass. You didn't get to see the entire offense versus defensive alignments, how they both change back and forth before, then during the play, the audibles like a chess match on both sides of the line of scrimmage. The receivers were running beautiful intricate full-field patterns. How they harmonized their patterns with each other, often picking off a defensive back in rhythm. On TV, you didn't get to see the defensive schemes, how the defensive halfbacks and safeties checked off on their zone-coverage assignments at full speed while covering speedy receivers. And let's not forget the best thing about live games over TV—no onslaught of mind-numbing commercials!

Sitting back in my seat after clicking the cheerleader photo, I enjoyed the roar of the crowd as the Dolphins kicked off and the fact that an usherette just took our orders for beers and hot dogs. That's service.

"I'll be right back, Mr. Walsh."

"Where you going?"

"I'm going to photograph the first play of the Super Bowl. Don't go anywhere."

"Where'm I gonna go? I can't walk. Haven't you noticed?"

Sheesh. Lay the guilt trip on me, why don't you. Anyway, I slid down to where the 49ers set up for their first play. And snapped the following shot:

"How that work out for you?" Mr. Walsh asked upon my return.

"Well, the play was all right. Joe tossed a perfect pass to Freddie Solomon in the flats."

"And it bounced off his chest, incomplete," he countered.

"I know. I'm sure I caught the ball, Joe's first pass, in midair. It wasn't a successful play, but it was the first."

I translated his shaking of the head to mean, "Who cares?"

Miami shut the Niners down and took over. The Miami offense, famous for their passing prowess, surprised everyone by opening up with a running attack. Coach Walsh, who besides the West Coast Offense further revolutionized football by putting in situational defenses, kept continually substituting his defenses onto the field depending on the situation. He used different defenses utilizing different personnel, and this innovation completely changed how the NFL played defense to this day.

Legendary Coach Don Shula of Miami stifled a smile on his sidelines. Coach Shula had caught Bill Walsh flat-footed by shifting into a no-huddle offense, a blitzkrieg if you may. Most fans in attendance never saw a no-huddle, hurry-up offense before. Miami never used it during the game all season. Surprise!

Miami promptly drove right down the field. But the Niner D stiffened and held the Dolphins to a field goal. Miami went up 3–0.

Sure enough, as Coach Walsh's dad told me he would, the 49ers counterpunched. They came out using Bill's choreographed, memorized script and marched straight down the field like a hot knife cutting through butter. Montana mercifully ended the initial drive by mercurially passing thirty-three yards to a wide-open, seldom-used, obscure reserve halfback, Carl Monroe, for the game's first TD. San Fran 7, Miami 3. I explained what was happening to Bill Sr. He cracked his first smile of the day, finally loosening up a bit after our section finished cheering the touchdown in our unique over-the-top manner. He appreciated my sharing of inside knowledge of the game. I explained as Miami's offense came back out on to the field, how Miami had an excellent hurry-up offense and how they felt this was a great way to score. Bill Walsh Sr. laughed hysterically after my insightful explanation.

"What did I miss?" I asked surprised and a bit annoyed. After all, I'm generously helping him out with my football acumen, and he's laughing?

"Aren't you watching?" he asked. "Why did that sly ol' silver fox from Miami do that?" he asked, referring to Miami's coach, Don Shula.[21]

"To speed things up like I just said."

He peered at me through glasses so thick, his eyes look big and milky. "No, dummy, he caught my son offguard. Bill can't get his slow-ass, too-big-to-stop-the-pass defense off the field. All because Miami doesn't have a huddle to slow things down. Thus, Bill has no opportunities to exchange players or to put in his speedier smaller pass defenders. Look at Hacksaw Reynolds."

I threw my binocs on him. Poor Hacksaw trying to cover Miami's roadrunners—the famous Mark brothers, Duper and Clayton, cutting over the middle. Hacksaw's getting burned.

"They're gonna score. Just you watch," Mr. Walsh Sr. said.

He was spot on. Don Shula caught Coach Walsh completely off guard and scored, dominating the first quarter in time of possession to take the lead 10–7. The seventeen total points set a Super Bowl record for most points in the first quarter. Miami looked unbeatable.

"So you think Coach Shula has a better game plan today than your son?"

"You allergic to listening? I told you Bill's a counterpuncher. He'll take what you throw at him, adjust, and come back even stronger. Just you watch."

Second quarter, the boxer counterpunched. He went with a nickelback defense[22] and left them on the field. This helped stop Marino's no-huddle offense. Plus, adjusting to the style used by Miami's O line, Defensive Coach Seifert started using stunts and unleashed a furious pass rush that got to Marino. Fred Dean and Duane Board got into a contest to see who'd get to Marino first. They playfully argued

---

21 At the time of this writing this Hall of Famer is the winningest NFL coach of all time with 347 victories, has the second most Super Bowl appearances with 6 (Bill Belichick has 7), and coached the only undefeated team, the Dolphins, back in 1972.

22 Simply meaning he now had five defensive backs instead of four.

on the sideline about who was doing better much to the delight of the hometown fans who were in on it.

The Niners kept running this one particular play: Joe first telegraphed, then tossed a pitchout to Roger Craig running to the outside. Roger would inevitably get tackled for another loss.

Now I gave Mr. Walsh a taste of my smarts. "They keep running that same play. It goes nowhere every time," I moaned. "I wouldn't mind telling your son to stop calling it. It never works."

He shook his head in disgust. "Can't you see he's setting up the defense for later, you nincompoop?"

Nincompoop?

"You told me you knew the game," he said.

Ornery Bill Walsh Sr. had little patience for neophytes like me.

Sure enough, later in the quarter, Montana needed to convert a crucial key third down.

"Here it comes, boy, Bill's set 'em up like bowling pins perfectly. Get ready."

I did and whipped my 35-mm camera out.

And just as sure as the setting of the sun, Montana *faked* that same exact pitchout to Roger Craig. The Dolphins excited, thinking they knew what play was coming, went for the fake—hook, line, and sinker.

Walsh Senior roared with laughter at Miami's Coach Don Shula, yelling, "Watch the fake!"

Too late. Joe had them programmed. He ran right straight up the gut. Since I was prepared, thanks to Bill Walsh Sr., I snapped this shot right before Montana took off toward the goal line to put the Niners up 21–10 at the half.

Strike—touchdown 49ers.

One quickly came to understand where the Genius got his smarts. His dad. This guy *saw* the game at a different level from the rest of us. Where everyone else, especially me, watched a game of checkers, he observed a game of chess.

Bill Walsh Sr. showed me all this, plus the importance of reading the coaches' body language. In short, *seeing* like Don Juan in a Carlos Castañeda novel, seeing the big conceptual picture. Whoever watched a game through the coaches' eyes before?

I learned, albeit slowly. Numerous successful plays in the second half, like double reverses, were a direct result from setting up these plays earlier in the first half. Originally, I thought they were just unsuccessful plays. *Duh!*

One of the more interesting aspects, once you *see* the game—or in my case, once someone shows you the game—you come to realize the game is all about the deceit and trickery that the coaches put into their game plans. All rather fascinating. Like everything, life's secrets were easy to spot once someone shows them to you.

For example, Bill Sr. said, "Ah, good, the Niners lined up to run right side behind the tackle. Good play coming."

When they did just that, I asked, "How you always know what play's coming next?"

"You got those big binoculars hanging around your neck. See for yourself."

I stared at the wizened old wizard with the cap jammed down until they met his eyes and waited.

He said, "Can't you see the right tackle's hand on the ground?" he grumbled, appalled with me. "Look—every passing play, the tackle lightly grazes his fingertips to the ground when in his three-point stance. He's practically leaning backward. Running plays, he jammed his knuckles firmly into the ground so hard, they turned white. Thought you watched this team all year you said. We watchin' the same game here?"

"Maybe you should've let your son know this. What if Don Shula picked this up?"

"You don't think Shula's already picked this up?" he exclaimed, exasperated. "You have any idea how long Shula's been coaching? Twenty-five years?"

"But . . . but . . . if Shula knows this, why . . ." I stammered.

"Haven't I told you about setting up plays earlier?" He shook his head. *You lunkhead,* he must've thought. He tried from his chair to slap me upside the head, feisty ol' bugger. Sure enough, inside the red zone on Miami's sixteen-yard line, the lineman's knuckles crushed into the ground. I learned later Montana told him *just at that moment* in the huddle to change his stance *for that one play*. Instead of the telegraphed run, Montana play action-faked the run behind that tackle; the Dolphins went for the fake pouring into the line to stop the run; Montana, catlike, floating above the ground, quickly dropped back, catching Miami flat-footed and boom—he fired a laser, a sixteen-yard strike to a wide-open Roger Craig. Touchdown, Niners. Shula got outfoxed.

Anyway, you get the point. This happened throughout the game. The players used as so many chess pieces on the board. The Niners would be running, running, running plays until Miami put a running defense on the field.

Then SF suddenly switched to their West Coast Offense, stranding Miami's running defense on the field and opening up a blistering passing attack against Miami's *run* defense, turning the tables on what Miami tried in the first quarter. It was like watching a finely tuned orchestra with a genius conductor at the helm. Or should I say a boxer?

On defense, Old Man Walsh pointed out how the Niners disguised their defense, putting seven in the box then dropping back five or six defensive backs to cover Marino's targets. Meanwhile, their blitzing schemes made Marino's first Super Bowl appearance a most unpleasant experience. Dapper Dan had a hand in his face the entire day, and the Niner D constantly harassed him.

I got so excited watching the game inside the game, I threw my binoculars up, looking at details and asked, "Okay, what do you think your son's calling in *this* situation?"

No answer.

"Mr. Walsh? Mr. Walsh?" Why was the ol' coot not answering me?

"Potatoes," he finally answered in a muffled distant voice.

"What does that mean, sir? Potatoes?" I pressed. "That code for something? Mr. Walsh . . . *Mr. Walsh?*"

Still, no answer. I put my binoculars down, looked to my left toward him, and my jaw dropped. I spotted an empty seat. I yelled, "What the F!"

The father of the head coach of the San Francisco 49ers lumbered down the aisle screaming, "The potatoes are burning! The potatoes are burning! Get 'em the hell off the stove! The potatoes are burning!"

The entire disability area, loaded with both physical and severely mentally disabled people screamed in delight, waving their arms around frantically, shouting, and carrying on. Popcorn, nachos, and fluids filled the air.

Their caretakers yelled, "Settle down!" These unexpected outbursts in the middle of the play delighted them to the max.

Down the aisle, I'd scamper. After catching up with him, I said soothingly, "The potatoes are fine, sir. Let's get you back to your seat."

"But the potatoes," he whimpered.

These explosions continued sporadically throughout the game. "Boy," I whispered to another caretaker, "what's with these burning potatoes anyhow?"

It wasn't until *after* the game that I learned the secret of the damn potatoes.

Quickly, I'd sit Mr. Walsh back down into his wheelchair, his eyes watery and wild. I'd fix his plaid blanket back around his legs and adjust his 49ers cap into place.

"Okay, Mr. Walsh, it's second and ten. We just ran behind our guard Randy Cross for no gain, 5:33 still to go, second quarter."

He'd hunker down, focus, and take over again, quietly, fascinatingly narrating the game. I'd find myself once again absorbed in his narrative. This interesting little dynamic played out for the entirety of Super Bowl XIX.

I wondered mightily why no one in his family bothered warning me about this mystery *before* the game. Out of all those Walsh relatives, couldn't *one* of them have given me a heads-up? Turned out Bill Walsh Sr. suffered from Alzheimer's disease. Quite the surprise letting me learn this on my own. To this day, I can't believe no one shared this little secret with me. Surrounded by Walsh relatives throughout the day and not a single heads-up?

Anyway, back to the game. Insiders know defense wins championships. Our D spotted Marino those early two first-quarter touchdowns and then shut him down completely with the aforementioned defensive adjustments on the way to a 38–16 drubbing of the mighty Dolphins. San Francisco gained a Super Bowl record 537 yards. Wait, a *drubbing* was too soft for what the 49ers did to the popular Miami Dolphins. How about they *annihilated* them, or how about they *pulverized* them? Wait, I got it. The Niners *excoriated* or even *flayed* the mighty Dolphins in Super Bowl XIX in a blowout.

Randy Cross summed it up best to a live TV announcer, "Everyone came to see a spectacular offense, and the wrong one showed up."

San Francisco won their second Super Bowl. Joe earned his second Super Bowl MVP. He had his best season to date and led the league in both scoring and passing yardage. I'd say the defensive line who harassed Marino all game was runner-up MVP after Joe.

The 49ers finished the 1984 season as the most dominating team in NFL history with a record of 18–1. One measly missed field goal from a perfect record. I wonder if Ray Wersching often thinks about his missed field goal. He makes it, and the 49ers might have finished as the greatest undefeated team in history at 19–0. Much better than the 1972 Miami Dolphins' 14–0 season.

However, Wersching, with the Niners on their own measly twenty-yard line, missed it, and it became their only loss of the season by a lousy three points.

Ray Wersching[23] hilariously never looked up at the goal posts. He would jog onto the field looking down, his right hand on the holder Joe Montana's shoulder and would only finally look up as he sailed the ball through the goal posts, usually. Not that day.

But back to the 1984 Forty-Niners. They *must* include them in any conversations about the greatest team in NFL history. Roger Craig became the first back ever to crack the 1,000/1,000 club: 1,000 yards rushing and 1,000 yards receiving. The entire Niner organization and the City smartly partied heartily, deep into the San Francisco fog— champions once more, thus proving their first Super Bowl victory was no fluke.

After pushing Bill Walsh Sr. into the celebratory circle of his family, I enjoyed a quick refreshing glass of a bubbly Dom Perignon someone shoved into my hand. I said my goodbyes and walked off into the night. The Father of the Genius, who few knew existed, yelled, "Rick, you get back over here!" He stood, shaking but determined and with

---

23   According to a *San Francisco Gate* article written by Sam Whiting on Tuesday, April 21, 2009, Ray Wersching would eventually "be charged with four felonies alleging embezzlement of millions." His partner, who had a 50-50 share in Ray's insurance agency was "convicted and sent to federal prison for the crime of fleecing Farmers Insurance by the sum of $8.3 million." He was eventually exonerated but not his partner, and he also lost his business and his money. Poor Ray shanked that kick then his post-NFL career. Ray, however, retired with the 49ers after a ten-year stint with the franchise record for total points, field goals, and extra points.

great difficulty. We embraced in as damn fine a man hug as I ever experienced.

"Goodbye, Mr. Walsh and thanks for teaching me how to *watch* the game inside the game."

"Thanks for *watching* me." He smiled broadly and with a twinkle in his eye warned. "And don't let those potatoes sit too long on that stove. They'll burn, you know."

We both shared a fat laugh on that one. I never knew he knew what he was saying.

I looked around. The coast was clear. "You know, I gotta be honest," I whispered to him. "I feel a little sorry for Dan Marino."

"Oh, don't be," he said. "He's what, twenty-two? He'll be back for many Super Bowls before he hangs up his cleats."

Dan Marino never played in another Super Bowl for the remainder of his life. I never saw Bill Walsh Sr, this most interesting man, again. And I never watched the game of football the same way again either.

CHAPTER 19

'85: "RICE-A-RONI, THE SAN FRANCISCO TREAT"

THE FOLLOWING YEAR, 1985, SF had that damn hangover again. They finished 10–6 and were one-and-dones in the playoffs. The New York Giants kicked them to the curb in the first round. The Niners scored a measly three points that game. This became the big breakthrough year for the '85 Chicago Bears to win their one and only Super Bowl.

The Niners did, however, draft Jerry Rice with their number 1 pick in 1985.

1985, Midseason

The three of us loved it when R. C. stopped in the War Room for a cup of joe to tell us about the 49er practices.

Gunner asked, "Why does Coach Walsh keep playing that kid out of Mississippi State? He's dropped every pass thrown his way all season thus far and is killing the team?"

R. C. only grinned. "He's gonna be one of the all-time greats one day, son. Mark my words."

We three rolled our eyes. Tall Brad stuck in his two cents'. "No disrespect, R. C. but he sucks. Butterfingers. Also, the fans always booin' him gotta be killin' his confidence. They'd be best to cut him from the team and focus on other up-and-coming wide receivers."

R. C. looked at Brad with his eyes half closed. "Ronnie [Lott] tol' me that boy cried his eyes out when he be droppin' passes in those game.

How many today's players care that much? Let me tell you boys 'bout the practices and this rookie. Things you don't know."

Great, an R. C. story. They were the best. I refilled everyone's Styrofoam cups with the horrific-tasting coffee and tossed the sugar packs out onto the table. Gunner, who I presumed evolved from the endless seeds he chewed last year, tossed a pouch of shredded bubblegum on the table, resembling baseball players' chewing tobacco. We grabbed a pinch. That powdery pink bubblegum flavor was the best.

R. C. put his gigantic feet up on the table, kicked back, and sat a mile away. He regaled us with this tale: "In the practices, Montana and Matt Cavanaugh be throwin' passes to all the wide-outs. Jus' a regular drill, see? These here receivers, they'd be catchin' the ball and jus' flippin' it back to the ball boy like always. The ball boy, he'd run it back to the QBs who just kept on firing away. Routine, right?" He blew across the black sludge in his cup to cool it down.

"But this here rook from Bumfuck, Egypt, no, he didn't flip the ball back. He ran every ball he catches full speed down the field into the end zone. Then he hustled back and handed it to the ball boy. Now the veterans, they none too pleased seein' some rook tryin' to show 'em up. You boys know what I'm sayin'?"

We nodded, riveted to R. C.'s story as always.

"The coaches be lookin' at each other smilin'. The vets, they started givin' Jerry some flack. And then the strangest thing happened." He smacked his lips and sat up. "How come this coffee's always so damn awful?" He stared into it.

"We don't know. We tried everything. We don't even know why we bother drinking it before each game," I said.

Gunner reached into his inside jacket pocket and ever-so-slightly revealed the flask we used to pour into the mud to make it drinkable. He raised his brows, but I waved him off. R. C. was, after all, a big part of the establishment. Why chance it?

"Please continue," I said, handing him enough sugar packets so he could probably chew the coffee.

R. C. continued, "Well, I'd be damned if it wasn't the funniest thing I ever seen. Joe Montana fired a short pass to Johnnie [Taylor], and Johnnie run the ball all the way down the field just like the rookie. Next pass, Roger Craig, he do the same damn thing. Then Ronnie [Lott]—you know he be the real leader on this team—he and the defenders run all the way down the field tryin' to catch their asses. Now they all be doin' it, every pass, every practice. No wonder the Niners be leadin' the league in yards caught after the catch. Damn rookie goes out and revolutionizes—rev whole who shun azzes—the entire practices, all of 'em."

He stood tall, dropped the coffee in the trash followed by spit. He scrunched up his face and said, "I be goin' to see the Stevens boys and get me a real cup of coffee. Get this taste outta my mouth. See y'all later."

We immediately dumped more rum into our coffee and smiled. Gotta love that R. C.

I watched Jerry a lot closer after hearing that story. On December 9, against our rivals, the LA Rams, in front of a national viewing audience on *Monday Night Football*, I experienced his breakout game. That night, Jerry fixed his dropped pass problem by having a 10-catch, 241-yard game. When we had the ball between the forty-yard lines, I could really check out our new phenom closely from my spot at the bench. Such a pleasure. He became the NFC's rookie of the year. Then became the greatest wide receiver in history.

Now, how can I describe Rice in mere words? A Rice catch. I'm certain sports authors define it way better than I can. But I refuse to read other books about the 49ers. Why? I'm afraid consuming other stories about them would interfere with my own sweet very personal memories. But here goes.

Other wide receivers would *thump*, make the catch. Next, they would try to run if possible, maybe toss a fake turn after the catch. Usually, they were nailed on the spot, even the really good ones. Jerry was a totally different animal. He tacked on yardage after each catch. He ran his routes as smoothly as a hawk gliding on an air current, always snagging the ball in stride. Loved watching him run his razor-sharp precision routes over the years.

Montana would zip bullets toward him. But there was no *thump*, catch, then run. He cupped his hands in front of him; arms extended, let the ball hit same hands as he skated downfield. He somehow kept the momentum of the ball going. It never slowed down after he caught it. Jerry merely transferred the ball's speed and energy from the air into his outstretched hands, into his possession, so smoothly, all the while going like the Roadrunner cartoon. Thank God Tall Brad, who had been consistently bad-mouthing him, was no scout. But then again, only the genius of Coach Walsh would see enough talent to draft a skinny kid out of Mississippi Valley State University, an I-AA school, and off of everyone else's radar.

As Jerry's star rose to new prominence, my love life ran in the complete opposite direction. Finally, over JT's spurning me, I immersed myself into the San Francisco dating scene. What a disaster.

After the game, I took a young lady, Miriam, who lived in a beautiful Victorian house in the Haight-Ashbury District. She was gorgeous, quick to laugh, and had a sharp wit I admired. We had two dates so far, and this relationship looked promising. I took her out to a dance bar in San Rafael up in Marin County. Here she danced with me—and any other guy who asked her. When she danced twice with the same dude, I drained the remainder of my greyhound, flipped her off while she was looking at me from the dance floor, and slipped out the back door, never to see her again.

After the long discouraging drive home, I looked over my social network. Paulette, across the street, was convenient, but the fact that she had a young kid made that relationship difficult.

Barbara, who went by Bar, was cute as a button but despised any form of intimacy far as I could tell. She was not kinesthetic in the least.

The morning of December 10, 1985, I called each one, ended my charade of a love life, and broke off all engagements with the opposite sex. I lit a candle and put into my active Daytimers diary a vow of celibacy. I refused any longer to pour all those hours upon hours of trying to find the one. Instead, I would invest that newfound time and energy into my burgeoning career as a regional manager at FedEx, my daily workouts, and this part-time job with the 49ers.

The next day, December 11, 1985, on my birthday, now celibate, I felt free from burden while putting in a long work out at my fitness center in the Stonestown Shopping Mall in San Francisco.

In the parking lot, after a long, unhurried lunch, I popped the back hatch of my Mazda RX-7 and checked out the gift my parents mailed me. It was a ski sweater, so I tried it on. When my head popped out of the other end, I met my soul mate, Maureen. Our sports cars were parked next to one another.

We struck up a conversation and connected on every level. We had an incredible double date that same night with hippy Van and his significant other, Patricia, at Original Joes in the Tenderloin District, followed by a Johnny Winter concert at the Stone. Best birthday present ever.

Funny thing was Gunner also had a steady girlfriend. I met her when he threw that massive fundraising gala for some WASP charity in his upscale Pacific Heights neighborhood—which I attended as a single. I just didn't think him capable of holding down a relationship, and I'm not sure why.

Brad played the field, and he did well sneaking girls into Candlestick Park. He loved the singles scene. But I had just given up completely. The dating scene for me was horrendous. And right after giving up, right when I swore an oath of celibacy and would say no to any new opportunities no matter what, *boom*, there was a black sports car parked next to mine. Probably a lesson in there somewhere.

Thank God Joanne dumped me. Thank God the singles scene had left me scarred. And although I was celibate for less than twenty-four hours, I feel maybe that had something to do with it. Otherwise, Maureen and I would never have gone out. My mom always said ad nauseam, "Everything happens for a reason, Ricky."

How Maureen and I met I think tells an interesting story—for another memoir I've already written. As William Shakespeare said, "Journeys end in lover's meetings." We have been inseparable now for thirty-two years and counting, but I digress.

Nineteen eighty-five's awful 49er season was blamed on the Super Bowl hangover again. Not sure what the excuse was the following year in 1986. Personally, the year got off to a terrible start. On January 28, I watched from a corporate boardroom as the space shuttle *Challenger* exploded a mere seventy-three seconds after takeoff at 8:39 PST while I sipped my morning coffee. My company, FedEx paid a then-extraordinary sum of one million dollars for the shuttle to launch the first business communications satellite. As the shuttle program then went into a thirty-two-month hiatus, this had a direct effect on my full-time career.

My part-time career fared terribly as well. During the playoffs, the New York Giants whipped the lips off the Niners once again, this time waxing them 49–3. Thus, the '86 49ers were also one-and-dones and a disappointing team. They were back to the Forty-Effin-Niners. However, to rationalize this disappointment, they did offer a major lifelong lesson learned.

CHAPTER 20

'87: A LIFELONG LESSON LEARNED

The following year, 1987, three sports events occurred, all related to one another:

1. My alma mater, the Pennsylvania State University's football team, the Nittany Lions, won their second National Championship in front of the most widely viewed audience of all time. They defeated the heavily favored Miami Hurricanes led by Heisman Trophy winner Vinny Testaverde whom the Nittany Lions intercepted a stunning five times. We are!

2. Vinny Testaverde was then selected as the top pick in the 1987 draft by the hapless Tampa Bay Buccaneers. This made their current quarterback dispensable. The Team of the Eighties traded some draft picks for said disposed quarterback who turned out to be none other than a future Hall of Fame quarterback—a fella by the name of Steve Young.

3. The Niners had perhaps the greatest regular season during their dynasty, had the best record in the NFL, and set records for having the best offense *and* the best defense in the same season. More importantly, they provided me and countless others with an all-important, life-sustaining lesson. One I'll never ever forget.

THE WHITE-HOT, 13–2 Forty-Niners roared down the stretch. On December 14, 1987, before a national audience on *Monday Night Football*, they had a date with the loud, brash defending Super Bowl champion—Chicago Bears with their heralded flex defense and unstoppable Walter Payton–led running attack. Once again, the *Chicago Tribune*, the *Chicago Sun-Times*, and the Bear players themselves provided plenty of quips for pregame locker room material. Once again, the 49ers answered on the field of play. Action speaking louder than words to coin the old cliché.

"Hey, who you calling a finesse player? What was that about you being all meat and potatoes and street tough? And we were just a bunch of quiche-eating fags? Did I hear that right? C'mere. *Bam*! You want some more of this? *Smack*!"

The Niners took the NFL's premier team, just one year removed from the Super Bowl, out to the proverbial woodshed. Third-year veteran Jerry Rice, coming into his own, tied two NFL receiving records he'd later shatter. As the Niners did throughout the eighties—they simply owned Da Bears and obliterated the visiting former champions. The Niners punctuated the thorough beating by hanging the hallowed bagel on Da Bears' side of the scoreboard, 41–0. What a rout.

I made sure I wore my golden 49er jacket to all my business conventions, and yes, there was no more teasing. The 49ers were back, Jack.

Then SF crushed the Falcons 35–7.

Next, the Niners annihilated their in-state rivals, the LA Rams, by a score of 48–0. Trust me, it could've been worse, but Coach showed mercy. The spectacular season was highlighted by Joe Montana winning the passing title and Jerry Rice breaking the all-time receiving record by hauling in twenty-two touchdowns. SF led the league in both most yardage, 5,987, and was the crème de la crème among league defenders, allowing a stingy 4,095 total yards all season. Therefore, they had football's best offense *and* defense, a rare feat in any year, a sure sign of dominance heading into the '87 playoffs. San Francisco also owned home field advantage throughout the playoffs because of their superior record. They were heavily favored by the sports books to go all the way.

San Fran earned a first-round bye and hardly cared that their first playoff game would be the winner of a silly wildcard game between a subpar Minnesota Viking team versus the New Orleans Aints. Everyone said this was the best Niner team ever, even better than the '84 Super

Bowl champions. I agreed. The total combined score of their three playoff games was a jaw-dropping 124–7 for God's sake.

Gunner, Tall Brad, and I relaxed in our usual seats before the first playoff game in the War Room. El Capitán had us coming in earlier for playoff games. Going through our rituals, we picked the teams we thought would win using Vegas's odds. We'd circle a team for each game and call them into my bookie, a kid I met in my classes named Jimmy Ruiz[24] during my graduate program at San Jose State.

We didn't bet much. It was fun, but it rolled up to some impressive winnings. We kept rolling over our winnings week after week and kept the secret pot of gold among ourselves since money was tight in those days. What, with Black Monday on everybody's minds. On October 19, the global stock market had crashed.

I would listen to KCBS's *John Madden* show. He'd visit teams each week before the games and tell his audience how well the team looked at practice. Were they psyched? In synch? Were they prepared? Were they bickering? Listless? From my four years of high school ball and my 1.25 years of college ball, I knew one thing: how you practiced that week had a direct correlation to how you played that week.

The 49ers game was hard to pick. First, we had to look through our obvious bias. Secondly, since the golden helmets were having a golden year, they gave up a ton of points each week called the spread. Before the Vikings' game, you had to give up an astonishing 18 ½ points if you bet San Francisco.

Whenever R. C. Owens stuck his head into our War Room, we'd want to know how the 49ers looked at practice all week.

"How they look?" we asked R. C. on his visit as he poured himself a cup of the black sludge then listen as he complained about it. He always made a cup with the creamer and the sugar but never a once consumed it after his initial sip. He'd always say, "Great, man. The Niners looked great."

---

24   The following year, Jimmy got very popular. We were all winning, and the money he held became quite high. He suddenly and quite shockingly not only dropped out of school but also disappeared with our bread, never to be seen again. Did he enroll in a graduate program just to scam us?

"Terrible," he warned this time, however. "I don't think I'd pick 'em, not that I'm a bettin' man, mind you."

"Of course not," we always answered in unison to this ritual. "But what's wrong? Someone injured?" Injuries were always valuable inside information.

"No, they be all-overconfident, man, all of 'em. They be goofin' off and slackin'. Coach's hair can't get no whiter. He's pissed off at them for takin' the game so lightly."

"I'm layin' off of 'em," Gunner said, and we agreed.

"They'll win by two scores," I said, but covering 18.5? Maybe not.

On January 9, at Candlestick Park, I could *see* it in the pregame locker room, on the field, everywhere I looked, Gunner and Brad too. The nonchalant Niners were not ready for this game. Yeah, hindsight was 20-20, but this was seen with *fore*sight, not hindsight.

We three watched from my comfortable spot near the bench during their pregame warm-ups. Watched R. C. shaking his head as he watched them goofing off.

"You could tell they ain't giving the Vikes *no* respect," R. C. said. "None."

"Why should they?" Brad, who can be a dunce at times, said after announcing the time from his damn Mickey Mouse watch again even though no one asked. "Not only has Vegas installed San Francisco as 18 ½ point favorites—as high as it gets in the NFL before the bet comes off the board—but the Vikes lost three of their last four games. I mean, c'mon."

Gunner added, "This is Niner weather today. Wet, foggy, and muddy. On top of all that, Minnesota's starting QB pinched a nerve. They're starting their backup quarterback—Wade Wilson. I laid the points and picked SF."

"That's a lot of points. I laid off." I blew into my reddened hands. "My prediction is this: the Vikes would surprise the overconfident 49ers. Even take an early lead, but once the Niners woke up, they may maul and mutilate mediocre Minnesota. San Francisco possesses so much more superior firepower than the Vikings, it's not even funny."

He agreed for once and proceeded with his bizarre ritual of power-eating gum, shoving an entire pouch of Big-League Chew directly into his face until he resembled a human chipmunk.

In truth, Minnesota ended the season playing dismally. Sports pundits *demanded* an end to the wild card system because riff-raff like this now slithered into the playoffs. The Vikings making the playoffs embarrassed the entire league. Everyone sensed San Francisco would blow them out the Golden Gate and into the bay before halftime.

Coach Walsh certainly sensed this overconfidence. He screamed at his players while prowling the sidelines. He's usually *way* too cool to drop to that level.

Well, "On any given Sunday, any NFL team can beat any other team," Bert Bell, former NFL commissioner, famously said.

Game time, the heavy underdog Vikings came out hungry and on fire. Minnesota's Anthony Carter had a career game with ten catches for a playoff record of 227 yards to lead the Viking offense. Joe Cool, who all season led comeback after comeback, had the worst game of his career, proving anybody can have a bad game. First time I'd ever seen him have a bad game. The first time he had a bad game in the playoffs.

The worst part? Seeing an ineffective Joe Montana get embarrassingly and— as a shock to every player and fan—get yanked out of the game, replaced by his heir apparent, Steve Young.

Steve valiantly tried to rally them back by scoring one TD himself and throwing for two others, but it was all for naught—Mighty Casey had struck out. The wild card Vikings upset the heavily favored, arguably the best of all Forty-Niners teams, 36–24 in one of pro football's most stunning upsets of all time. It will always be in the top-ten list of most shocking sports upsets of all time. Walsh would go on to say this loss, "Was the most traumatic experience I ever had in sports."

All of us were blown away. I wrote diligently in my 49er logbook, smoke coming off my pen. I made an *intense* vow. Never would I let myself get that overconfident, *ever*. Never was a player finer than the Niner who ended up with a shiner. Got to be mentally prepared. I have to say, that lesson has stuck with me for*ever* like white on rice. Experience once again being the best of teachers.

Next week's playoff plans had to be canceled—including our hotel rooms overlooking a pool near Jack Murphy Stadium in postcard-perfect San Diego. Bummer.

I had thus far been to two Super Bowls, one in the sub -38-degree Silver Dome in Detroit, Michigan—sheesh—and the other I could have walked to, in foggy Stanford Stadium right down the road. I *so* wanted to spend time in tropical San Diego, but "the little guys" from Minnesota had shaken the NFL world. Damn you, Murphy—law, not the stadium.

Nineteen eighty-seven proved to be a bizarre season anyway. Why? Because once again we actually worked. There was a twenty-four-day player strike—three games. The team picked up SCABS, replacement players, to discontinue work stoppage and play the games again. Getting them from the busses into the Stick meant we once again provided protection.

We were known as the San Francisco Phony Niners and played teams like the New Orleans Saint Elsewheres and Seattle Sea-scabs and the Washington Scabskins. Again, I found myself ducking from bottles, batteries, and blame. Flying ketchup bottles and baggies filled with the unmentionable were not uncommon. But we scurried these guys from bus to gate. Eighty-five percent of the NFL players refused to cross the picket lines, and the ones that did were heavily ostracized. This resulted in a civil war within the NFL. Teams like the Washington Redskins had 100 percent of their players hold out. Coach Gibbs told them, "Either go up the hill as a team or go down the hill as a team—but stay as a team." They did.

The Dallas Cowboys, however, splintered when their stars Randy White, Tony Dorsett, quarterback Danny White, and Ed "Too Tall" Jones crossed the picket line. Team President Tex Schramm created this dissension on purpose by threatening to take away retirement annuities.

On *Monday Night Football*, October 19, 1987, Coach Gibbs proved that team unity defeats a team of individual stars. The Redskins, 100 percent SCABs, defeated the heavily favored Cowboys who had close to twenty regular starters 13–7 in yet another one of the biggest upsets in history.[25] The Scabskins[26] won all three of the replacement player games, which proved to be crucial in Washington winning the Super Bowl that season. Fans sang, "Hail to the Scabskins." They attained cult status.

Dallas, mired in ugly dissension, was never the same. They missed the playoffs, finishing 7–8. The owner, Jerry Jones, fired Tom Landry in ugly fashion. Tex Schramm resigned among the turmoil as president. He stated, after getting blown out at home against the lowly Falcons 21–10, that "this is probably the lowest I've ever been in my career, my twenty-nine years with the Cowboys."

Our spoiled owner Eddie DeBartolo, looking at a third consecutive year without a Super Bowl, went ape-shit. Not winning the Super Bowl equated to a complete failure of a season. Blaming Coach Walsh, as was common protocol with owners not quite getting it, stripped the president title away from Coach Walsh. Ouch.

That stung the professor, who also took the blame for the upset from upper management and the press. "Why was his team not ready?" they asked. Yet none tried harder than he in not letting them act so complacently, but '88 was so different for me.

It was different for the entire organization, which was sinking faster than a leaking boat filled with anchors.

---

25   Incredibly, during the game, Ed Rubbert, the efficient SCAB QB, went down in the first quarter with an injured shoulder. No way would a replacement team be two-deep at QB, right? Yet obscure Tony Robinson got the MNF audience excited by replacing Rubbert and going an amazing eleven of eighteen passing for 152 yards to win the game versus Danny White, star QB of Dallas! After the regular players returned a week later, Robinson went back to jail from whence he came on loan, to serve another four years and four months for a cocaine conviction. Unreal.

26   Despite going 3–0 with an all-replacement player team and defeating other NFL teams with regulars, they were not given Super Bowl rings until Tuesday, June 12 at 11:15 a.m. Sad, right?

CHAPTER 21

'88: ONE FOR THE ROAD

AUGUST 6, 1988, the big preseason game, the Battle by the Bay

SF versus the now new non–Bay Area, LA Traitors, uh, Raiders. After last year's hugely disappointing finish, I called for a meeting with El Capitán. The smoke cloud was so thick in his office, I thought it might rain any second.

I said to my supervisor, "Out of respect for you, El Capitán, I came here personally to officially resign after this game. You got someone you want me to show the ropes to, now's the time. Especially that gnarly Joe Montana escape maze after each game." I tossed my badge on his cluttered desk and felt an unexpected wave of sadness. "I'll turn my uniform in after the game."

He Who Never Smiles asked, "Why?"

"It's no fun any longer. Everyone's all pissed off about last year. Eddie D. demoted Coach Walsh. Rumors flew rampantly that this'd be Coach's last season. Joe's health's an issue. Even R. C., the eternal optimist, is down. Good time to split."

"Not a good enough answer. Every season's a lifetime on its own. You know that. This is a new year."

"Well, one more thing. I live in Santa Monica now. I relocated. My company—"

"You still working for FedEx?" he interrupted.

"Yeah, I run the LA branch now, and I relocated."

"Got a problem getting here?" He lit a cigarette and blew smoke rings. Guy had talent.

I looked up, thinking, then said, "No, not really. FedEx has its own airline. I simply jump seat to Oakland for free. If they don't have an available flight, I wear my preboarding tag and go straight to Gate E. Hop on PSA or AirCal. Takes a half hour to land, another half hour to get here, so really, the commute's fine."

"What those airlines charge these days to go LAX–Oakland?"

"Thirty-eight bucks."

"Well, give me the receipts from now on, I'll reimburse you. And you'll get fifteen dollars toward lunch. You pay for parking?"

"No, that's free at the airports."

"So, problem solved." The bony boss extended the palms of his hands upward.

What's with this guy? "Well, there's more. I got married three months ago. Bought a nice place down there not far from the Santa Monica beach and busy fixin' it up. Just got back from my honeymoon in fact."

"Where'ja go?"

"Bellagio by Lake Cuomo in the Italian Alps. Rained every day. We had cabin fever from being stuck in our room all day. However, the wife said she's gonna give me a chubby baby, and well, you got a ring on your finger—you know how it is. So yeah, I hereby officially resign."

He didn't answer at first, just locked on to my eyes. "Sorry. I cannot accept your resignation at this time."

That knocked me for a loop. This was after all a part-time job. More like a hobby, really. How could he stop me from quitting a rinky-dink job?

"Look," he continued. "We need you this year. You know where they buried the skeletons, how the mysterious tunnels run throughout the bowels of the Stick. I trust you with the plum assignments, like picking up the NFL Commissioner at the airport, guarding Bill Walsh's dad, getting celebrities to and fro. You know when to allow and, more importantly, not allow those pecker-heads into the locker room. It'll take more'n a game to show someone all that."

"I already told my wife the only reason I came today was to resign in person. It's set in stone. No way can I give you another year. My wife would kill me. Impossible."

"Listen to me, kid. Go out on top—after this season. What happened last year's over and done. Didn't you always complain about the two Super Bowls you worked, one in frigid Detroit and the other down the road in the fog? This one's played in South Beach, Florida, Joe Robbie Stadium, a tropical climate, just like you wanted."

Now how in the hell did he know I was saying that? Still, this might be only the second time we ever actually *talked* to one another.

"Yeah, El Capitán, that *had* been the dream. But the 49ers have been one-and-dones the past three seasons. You realize all three years none of our stars—Roger Craig, Jerry Rice, nor Joe Cool—have scored a single point? Why you think, especially now with the team so down and coming apart at the seams, that we'd be going to a Super Bowl?"

The Ghost of Christmas Future pointed a long bony skeletal finger at me. Then he added special effects to the haunting scene. White smoke billowed through both nostrils. The wind, all creepy like, howled outside.

"I guarantee it," he said in an icy voice. "I've been here long enough to know."

He grabbed his unfiltered Camel from atop the pile in his green glass ashtray, inhaled a final lungful, gave the required short cough, chortled, then squished his truck driver into the heap of cigarettes. They lay curled up like dead soldiers on a battlefield. "Plus, I got some new juicy assignments for you." He suddenly stood, tall and skinny. "We good, Lieutenant?"

Bewildered, I also stood and shook his extended nicotine-stained hand. "We're good." I grabbed the badge he handed me and looked him in the eye. I think he tried to smile, but his dried face refused to allow it.

I felt relieved about leaving his office, able to breathe healthy air once more. Thank God, this uniform encased my body within. The miracle fiber—polyester—had me wrapped tighter than a package. It protected me from the toxic poisons. Cotton clothing has pores, and the smoke would've reached my body, but nothing penetrated this polyester armor.

Nevertheless, how in the hell could a guy running a security outfit guarantee a Super Bowl? Furthermore, how—hey, what just happened?

How did I get talked into another year? Whoever heard of someone not accepting a retirement, especially from a part-time job?

My 1988 regular and final season started. The Forty-Effin-Niners sank straight into a nasty funk. Their spirit dropped faster than presidential candidate Michael Dukakis's numbers in the recent polls. That Viking loss put San Fran into a reverse tailspin. SF knew they could have defeated those guys ninety-nine out of a hundred games. The saddest part was this: I'll go to my grave saying last year's team was as good as or better than the famous '84 Niners who decimated the Dolphins. No 49er team was ever better at the end of the season than that team, where every position clicked on all cylinders. Poetry in motion on both sides of the line of scrimmage. Regardless, because of overconfidence, they lost.

Try as they may, they could not escape the vortex pulling them down toward Dante's Inferno. Fans, either fuming from last season's embarrassment or still locked into the lockout, booed a team that only yesterday was beloved on the entire peninsula and could do no wrong.

The professor, Bill Walsh, was royally pissed off. His boss, Eddie Debartolo Jr., expected a Super Bowl each and every season from Walsh or he deemed the season a failure. Three years have now gone by with no Super Bowl trophy. The press fixated on his publicly stripping of Bill's title as team president, which had to be a humiliation. What have you done for me lately?

That expectation was apparent everywhere. Right up front, veterans told rookies joining the team, "We drafted you for one reason: help us win another Super Bowl."

Coach Walsh took last year's loss especially hard. The perfectionist was extremely upset because he warned his *trusted* veterans: "You're getting sloppy and lazy" and "You think you could just throw your uniforms out there on the field and win."

"Don't worry, Coach, once the game starts, we'll be ready to play. We'll be sure and get the others ready too," they promised.

No, they didn't. They didn't keep their promise. The players let him down, or as I always have said over and over again ad nauseam, "A word spoken was never broken."

Walsh's trust in them was irrevocably broken. Now more boxer than genius, he struck back with a fury. The vets found themselves in heated battles with rookies and junior players to keep their starting positions. When they went offsides, they found their gluteus maximus firmly planted on the bench. Mistakes were *verboten*, fines abundant. Walsh traded players from previous Super Bowls for younger talent. Veterans, unceremoniously, were simply cut. Gravitas clung in the air tighter than a wet T-shirt.

This mutation of the new order was nowhere more prevalent than the bitter highly publicized battle for the leadership: the starting position of quarterback of the prestigious San Francisco 49ers between Saint Joe Montana and—cut to the Eagles song, "There's a New Kid in Town"—Steve Young.

Many vets, highly angered, felt benching Joe was sacrilegious. Others said, "If Coach goes with Steve, just keep your head down and play."

Coach Walsh, in his genius ways, stripped everyone down bare to the lowest common denominator, making it painfully clear, there were no stars on his team, not anymore. Each star fought to keep their job. Players were PO'd in this once-jovial locker room after games.

A pleasant memory of mine was walking around the locker. Everybody was new, fresh. Bill Ring, in his jock strap, hopped up on a bench and fired a bar of Ivory soap as if it were a football to Keena Turner who caught it. Bubba Paris moved in for the tackle, and everyone piled on to the ringing of laughter.

Cut to today, and after practice the players slammed their helmets into lockers. Instead of laughter, f-bombs were exploding, water coolers destroyed, and I mean pulverized. If you ever get reincarnated, do not come back as a water cooler. After games, these things got obliterated.

RICK PUCCI

"The team spirit is being severely tested," Gunner announced as I entered the War Room before a game in the middle of the '88 season. Not once have I entered this room before these two early birds.

I sniffed the putrid air. "What's wrong with you guys? Can't you smell the coffee's burning?"

The room with neither windows nor fresh air smelled worse than ever, the pea-green walls now peeling. Magazines and newspapers were strewn throughout the war room. "Ah, good to be home."

Making a fresh pot of the world's cheapest coffee, I said, "Nothing splits a team in two like a good quarterback controversy. You now have a different leader in two separate camps."

"R. C. tol' me, 'You see a lot of divide-and-conquer strategies deployed between the vets in the Montana camp and the new up-and-comers in the Steve Young camp. The fact that these two future Hall of Famers remained friends is a testament to the human spirit.'"

Gunner offered me his pouch. I do love the flavor of bubblegum. Why can't all gum have that great bubblegum flavor? I reached in. Suddenly horrified, I reeled my hand back faster than an optical laser beam.

"Are you outta your mind!" I screamed. "You crazy?"

Gunner smiled and shoved a thick bushy wad of chewin' tobacco into his pie hole.

"Now you chew tobacco?" I asked incredulously. Guy just had to be shoving something into that grinning face at all times. I continued. "What kills me is you're an executive downtown. You wear a suit 'n' tie to work, have a beautiful girlfriend, and you do this?"

"Nah." He spit thick brown syrupy juice into his empty Coke bottle. "Like you, bro, this is my alter ego. I only dip when here." He pulled his cap even lower, past his eyebrows. Then he read from the *Chron* while constantly and annoyingly clearing phlegm from deep inside his throat.

Today's *Green Pages*: "'Time to rebuild the team. The rest of the NFL has finally caught up to the West Coast's pass first, run second offense.'"

With a puffed-out left check, he read another article while grossing us out. "This one sanctimoniously said, 'Joe Montana is now officially a has-been due to his recent injuries.' Then there was this: 'The dispirited Niners found themselves at six wins and five losses, struggling, and looking to miss the entire playoffs. Even worse, they lost three of their last four games and four out of their last six. However, it was the teams they lost to that had heads hanging and helmets slamming to the ground.'

"'These were losses to the absolute worst teams in the NFL: Da Bears, whom the Niners owned all decade, to Phoenix—the laughing stock of the league and of course, last week, in the once upon a time Battle of The Bay—they stunk up the field, losing to the hated LA Traitors in a sloppy contest. The Raiders kicked three field goals to San Fran's single field goal in a 9–3 stinker.'"

That *was* a hard game to watch. I thought about El Capitán's guarantee. What a con job.

Brad, rolling a huge number, said, "Coach Walsh, man, he's just livid with this team. It all stems back to that horrible upset loss to the Vikes last year, how his vets let him down."

"But there's still hope," I chimed in, playing the role of the eternal optimist yet filled with doubt. "We witnessed another single play go down into forever 49er lore. They're now calling Steve Young's October 30 game-winning run against the Vikes the Run to go with the Catch.[27]"

"And the Amputation[28]" Brad added, cracking us up.

"You guys see the highlights of Steve's run? Unreal," I said.

Paul Zimmerman, a famous sportswriter who covered the NFL for forty-eight years, in a *Sports Illustrated* article along with a rundown tackle by Lawrence Taylor, called it, "The greatest play I've ever seen.

---

27   And later, the Drive

28   Brad was referring to Ronnie Lott. In April 1986, to avoid the long recovery time that would have followed reconstructive surgery, he famously had his broken pinkie finger amputated rather than miss the season. He then joined his teammates and gave them a spiritual lift.

Steve Young of the 49er's 49-yard gallop left Vikings tacklers all over the field."[29] Here's a URL of it below.[30]

"Fans booed Steve lustily all game as he stood in for an injured revered Joe. Then by the end of the game, Steve was receiving a standing O. Bizarre," Gunner said then spit. Ew.

Two other part-timers slipped into our room, nodded to Brad, and sat by his side. He fired up his bomber, in a windowless room no less. El Capitán could burst in any minute. I think the weed's getting Brad goofy. I bailed. Besides, I suddenly had a theory I needed to run past R. C.

I found R. C. as calm as the Pacific Ocean in May, hanging out at his usual spot alongside the bench, intently watching the team run through their drills. The weather was cool, fifty-one degrees, wet, foggy, misty, with a slight rain—just fine for Forty-Niner football weather.

"*Monday Night Football*," R. C said, "is really sumpin'."

I looked up at the tall hombre. I loved R. C. After a slump, he was back into his always-positive mood and, as a former star player, always with the insight.

We looked up and around at the NFL's oldest stadium under the lights and quietly just kept right on looking. The sea of red, the Kelly-green grass, the crowd participating with the Gold Rush's cheers, the Miner Niner Mascot running around in crazed fashion, the foggy mist racing past the stadium lights. No one was bored.

Plenty of shade was thrown at Candlestick back in the day. Pitcher Stu Miller was blown off the mound during the 1961 All-Star game and charged a balk. Grounds crews carried batting cages during batting practice back after they were lifted and dumped in the outfield by wind gusts. There was the infamous Croix de Candlestick pin, showing the SF symbol capped with snow and included the Latin slogan "Veni, Vedi, Viverde." ("I came, I saw, I survived"). These pins were proudly displayed by several Burns Security guards. They were given to the

---

29   *Sports Illustrated*, volume 127, no. 7, 9/14/17. p.126.

30   https://www.youtube.com/watch?v=9O5fXUOAvoY

proud fans who stayed for entire extra innings during Giant night games.

However, old venerable Candlestick Park[31] had its charm, especially during night games. Also, I knew this was my final MNF game working the bench. Thus, the game had sentimental value.

After about seven minutes of silence, I said, "The sea, once it casts its spell, holds one in its net of wonder forever, Jacques Cousteau."

"Jock who?" R. C. asked.

"Never mind." I looked up at him. I looked up to him in several ways and simply smiled. I'll miss R. C.

He said, "Tonight's must-win game here at the Stick, before a national TV audience, man. You can feel the excitement buzzin' in the soles of your feet."

The man had soul and not just in his feet. I too felt the buzz. You heard it, smelled it, felt it. Candlestick Park owned that distinctive hum as well. All veterans heard it. The barbecue smoke and the hot dog smell from the parking lot tailgates poured into the stadium.

I puffed out a lungful of air. "You see, R. C. I got me this here theory I came up with from my thought experiment."

He giggled that little giggle of his. "You been thinkin' about this awhile, I see. Lay it on me, my brother."

"Well, I kept thinking the Genius has to be up to something, right? He's too cerebral just to be pissed off all the time. Well, here it is, plain and simple: Coach Walsh has morphed into Vince Lombardi."

"Say what?"

"The professor's gone, replaced by a tyrant. His boxer side's come out, barking at his players no matter how well they performed. He's causing friction between the quarterbacks, plus every other spot on the

---

31   On October 17, 1989, Candlestick Park stood tall as it heroically held its own during the one and only Bay Area World Series between the Giants and the As. Because of its unique architecture where entire sections rolled during the Loma Prieta earthquake, measuring 7.1 on the Richter scale, not a soul was injured. The Stick protected everyone while just outside its borders, the Nimitz Freeway and portions of the Bay Bridge collapsed, causing numerous fatalities.

team on purpose, bringing out the competitive nature of man. All a part of his master plan.

"Lombardi kept his foot on his player's throats for three-quarters of the season. When he released it near the end of the year, right about now, relieved, the players soared like hawks and won games by wide margins."

R. C. laughed heartily. "Mr. Lombardi coached while I played. My favorite story of Mr. Lombardi: he be screamin' at his undefeated Packers in the locker room, banging things around. All up in a rage, right? When guard Jerry Kramer says, 'But, Coach, we're up 24–0.'"

"I laughed, having heard that one. Lombardi then unleashed a barrage of expletives. To paraphrase the best coach in NFL history's retort to Kramer: 'There you go. Once you start thinking like that— and no longer performing to your potential—you are no longer fit to be champions.'"

"That's what I'm saying, R. C. When Vince pulled his foot off the Pack's collective throats, it gave them the positive reinforcement they craved, the mighty Green Bay Packer Machine peaked at the most opportune time. They would finish the season blowing away all remaining opponents. This strategy produced, along with those great Celtic teams, the best dynasty in sports history. Coach Lombardi won five championships doin' this."

"So, you sayin' Coach Walsh be stealin' a page from Lombardi's book? Hmph."

"He's been an angry SOB all season, R. C., with nary a hint of his fabulous sense of humor." I turned to face the crowd so it looked like I was working as kickoff time approached.

R. C.'s laughter sounded thunderous. "Remember when Coach Walsh disguised himself as a bellhop and wrestled with Montana over his suitcase when Joe got off the bus at the Super Bowl? Then he greeted the others? Not hearing no mo' stories like that, no, sir."

"He was a friend to no player this season. By the way, how they look this week at practice?"

"After puttin' up three whole points against the Raiders? Man, the entire team's so low, they could walk under a snake's stomach with a top hat on. They be killin' each other at practice, really goin' at it. Ronnie [Lott] called a players-only team meetin'. Most of the time, those things don't work. I'm tellin ya, they just don't. Not like in the movies. Oh, I know they sound good and all in the newspapers and to the press, but they don't work. This time, however—it did. I think. We'll see how this game starts. Washington needs this one just as bad remember, or they won't be defendin' no title. Be defendin' nuthin' if'n they lose tonight."

R. C. yawned. "I always yawn before big games. Helps me relax." Then he scrunched his face and added, "What'chu doin' down here on the field with us common folk anyway? You've ignored us all season. You missin' us?" He knocked my security cap off.

Picking my cap up, I turned and spotted our on-the-field stadium announcer, Bob Sarlatte. Friendly as ever, he wore that full grin spread across his face. You broke into a grin yourself just looking at the happy guy. He was checking out his pregame announcements he'd soon be doing live on *Monday Night Football*. Egads!

"Of course, I miss you guys. But El Capitán gave me another assignment."

"Another gravy one?" Bob enjoyed hearing about my various assignments.

"Yes, El Capitán said, 'After you leave the locker room, keep an eye on things up in the press box. Guard the MNF game announcers, Al Michaels, Frank Gifford, and Dan Dierdorf.'"

"Sounds fun," he said. "Sharp guys, all three of 'em."

"I know. I've been the invisible man up in the booth before. I only wish the public could hear their banter when their microphones were *off*. These guys were real characters."

"What's it like up there?" R. C. asked.

"The press box is like a beehive with little notes scurried in and out. Statistics were written down then sent back and forth physically to the outside MNF truck wired into the telecast. Statisticians in the truck immediately send up stats culled from listening to the announcers on air."

"In-ter-est-in', go on." R. C. rubbed his chin.

"Let's say, Giff is discussing—oh, I don't know—how well the Niners performed this year in the red zone versus last year. Okay? The Giff would quickly have red zone comparisons of the Niner teams of the past eight years handed to him."

Bob, listening in, said, "What's today? November 21, 1988? You'd think there'd be better technology around than writing stuff down and using sneaker-net. Who you ushering in to do the halftime segment?"

"Never know till the last minute, but I heard I got Joe Willie Namath tonight. Like me n' Montana, Joe's a fellow Pennsylvania boy. Which I always remind him about when he goes into his Broadway Joe bullshit."

Bob chuckled. "I'm sure you will. You ushered him before, right?"

"Working the press box this season, I ushered in all kinds of guests. They'd be anyone from a famous musician, actor, or a politician. If in fact it is Broadway Joe tonight, I'll simply escort him from his box seats to the press box. Joe's one of the few celebs who talks to guards. It'll be just Joe Willie Namath, me, and maybe I'll grab jealous Gunner if he's not too busy chewing or Tall Brad if he's not too busy puffing."

They both laughed.

"It's pretty low key," I continued. "Often, the star players would bring a wife or a significant other they were trying to impress. We'd keep the ladies in the wings but guard them nevertheless. But Namath's nothing like the entourages following some of the starlets I'd guard. Some of these divas who'd come up to the box, holy cow. Take Sally Kirkland. She introduces me to her entourage, and I'll never forget it. She just won a Golden Globes Award in 1988 for *Anna* and was nominated for Best Actress.

"She got her astrologist, her therapist, her shrink, her acupuncturist, her memoirist, her manicurist, her masseuse, her lifestyle coach, her dietician, her yada yada yada snore—a freakin' twenty-member posse. You always gotta remind them, 'Hey, keep it down. There's a live telecast going on.'"

Nobody said anything, so I continued, "By the way, John Madden and Summerall are *awesome*. Everyone looks at us guards as if we're invisible—which I'm totally cool with—but these guys are amiable to everybody. They're as clever, witty, and knowledgeable about the game off the mike as when on the air. They're regular season. MNF games are rare at the Stick. I'm really looking forward to working the booth, being with Al Michaels, Frank Gifford, and Dan Dierdorf who's hot right now and—"

R. C. reached down from a mile away and shook me out of my nonstop babble. "Ain't chu workin' the locker room no mo'?"

Dang. I looked at the field. The 49ers headed off the field toward the destination where I was supposed to be. The crowd roared under the black nightlights. I thanked the gentle giant and sprinted to my usual pregame assignment—manning the locker room door.

Inside, the room was beyond tense. A Monday night showdown with the current NFL champs. The 49ers had to win for survival. Same with the 'Skins. Whoever lost misses the playoffs—and millions of dollars in contract incentives. The executives would lose millions more in merchandising, TV ad revenues, and concession sales. It was a do-or-die situation for both squads.

Both Gunner and Brad bet the 49ers, coming off two straight losses, would lose big versus the defending Super Bowl champions and division-leading number one ranked Washington Redskins led by Coach Joe—three Super Bowl Rings—Gibbs. It made me sick knowing who they'd be rooting for deep inside.

Coach Walsh knew how to motivate before the big games. He mastered this technique before the Dolphins Super Bowl game. Smart coaches come and go in sports. However, the superior ones are rare. They know how to channel that unseen concept known as team spirit. It's an oft-heard phrase but seldom experienced. Herein lies the secret for coaches who win and remain. The *spirited* teams win games, not the most talented.

Well, Coach Walsh certainly *brought it* before Monday Night Football's game in spectacular fashion. He removed the foot from the proverbial jugular vein after having it planted there all year long. Or as Ronald Reagan famously said on October 28, 1980, when defeating Jimmy Carter in a presidential debate, "There he goes again."

He challenged their manhood. To paraphrase him from my notes:

"The defending champion Redskins aim to become the team of the eighties. They already wear two Super Bowl rings— the same as you, the San Francisco 49ers.[32]

"You guys aren't truthfully a six-win, five-loss bunch of has-beens, are you? No? What are you exactly then? Are you real men? Champions? Or just big boys inside? Each one of you knows. It's been three long seasons since we got back to the big dance, but tonight"—he made sure he had eye contact with his leaders—"tonight, we start our quest for number three. But only if you want it badly enough. Tonight's game is as important a game as this organization has ever had. If you are truly men, tonight, in front of a national audience, go out and prove what you're made out of in this do-or-die situation. There's no turning back. We lose, we're out. Don't lose. Win. Do whatever it takes."

The San Francisco 49ers burned their canoes on the shore and *had* to take the island or perish. The team spirit rose higher than I had seen in the past three years. Everyone in that locker room felt it pulsating through their veins. He threw down the challenge. Challenged their manhood. Inside the locker room, the Niners were back.

"Do it for your teammates. Do it for the city of San Francisco. Do it for the 49er Faithful who believe in you. Do it for yourselves. C'mon, fellas, bring it in."

They huddled as tightly as a clenched fist around a roll of quarters, around the professor, the Genius. He may have been a sonovabitch all season, but to a man, they loved him. Loved him! And I don't use the word *love* lightly. The huddle tightened further into a serious knot. He murmured something only they heard. It got stone quiet. Suddenly, the huddle exploded to a booming—"49ers! LET'S KICK SOME FRIGGIN'ASS!"

The golden helmets went on. Out they went through the unique tunnel in the traditional two-by-two march, which was all that could fit in that narrow tunnel leading out to the field. They puddled up on the

---

32   From 1981 to 1989, the Niners or the 'Skins represented the NFC in the Super Bowl an amazing seven out of nine years. Thus, the battle for supremacy.

other end of the tunnel and waited. Bob Sarlatte announced the starting lineup in his radio-perfect voice. One by one, the starters sprinted out.

The remainder of the team ran out afterward under the lights behind the steady sprint of the Genius in his white cardigan sweater matching his white hair, matching the white eagle soaring above, symbolizing the Great Spirit, flapping its wings in a full wingspan above the stadium ready to do battle with the enemy. The crowd roared in euphoric delight.

I know I'm alive when I *see and feel* this Great White Spirit, waving her majestic wings. This same spirit was seen/felt when the Beatles took the stage on the Ed Sullivan show for the first time in 1964. The teenyboppers screamed at full throttle as this spirit filled their pubescent veins and their every cell. They called it Beatlemania, but it was the Great Spirit inflicting them for the first time. The Father, the Son, and this the Holy Spirit.

When once together with my pal, Rhino Boy, a.k.a. Kris Mikkelson, we caught a Jethro Tull concert at Konocti Harbor, California, Ian Anderson launched into his flute solo during the song "With You There to Help Me," something happened. Ian caught the Spirit. He, laughing into his flute like a madman, using echo pedals, playing his ass off, singing, spitting, crying, "Why am I crying, I want to know?" It was so heartfelt and lovely that grown men openly wept in the audience and women shuddered.

Again, when immediately after graduation, when Joanne and I set out on the road in my 1965 LTD Ford with the V-8 engine, the nylon interior, and the hideaway headlights, leaving behind the old frozen snow country of Pennsylvania, going to California, "Going to California" by Led Zeppelin played over my FM. Unreal.

The Great White Spirit soared when I and my pal Rich Scharbach carved Lake Tahoe skiing Squaw Valley or Alpine Meadows or pounded Kirkwood's virgin snow. We sliced through said snow like two razorblades, blowing away younger skiers as if they stood still, letting Mother Nature's gravity pull us down the natural mountain fault line fast and effortlessly. If you so much as peeked to either side during your run, you'd see a blur, so you fixed your eyes back onto the Champaign snow and soared underneath the Great White Eagle.

The final and best example of soaring with that amazing Spirit was when it miraculously touched down inside the Olympic Village of the 1984 LA Olympic Games. It was truly an international hug fest. Everyone felt the White Eagle's presence. Every country's athletes and fans alike competing in peace and harmony felt it. Seeing an Israeli and an Arab athlete tightly hug each other after a tough competitive boxing battle, beautiful to experience.

Now, the Great White Spirit had arrived once more. It had been too long. Normally, the 9ers jogged onto the field. Not tonight. Now, under the golden helmets of champions, the San Francisco Forty Niners, finely tuned and at full efficiency, ensconced in that same Spirit, ran full speed, reborn in spirit, recharged from their lowest point in four years, which was scoring three measly points against the Raiders. Tonight, the phoenix rose from the ashes. They were alive in the moment.

We are not human beings having spiritual experiences. We are spiritual beings having human experiences.

I figuratively flew up the concrete ramp toward my press box assignment, ready to watch the game, full of glee, adrenaline pumping freely throughout my body, every syntax firing off energy. I just wanted to hit somebody.

Anybody who had ever played the game of football knows precisely what I'm saying. I meant this in a good way, not a violent way. There were just times when you needed solid competitive *contact*.

Yet while the Great Spirit soared above, death lurked below.

CHAPTER 22

DEATH AT THE STICK

RUNNING RATHER QUICKLY up the wide ramp, I spotted the Hogs from D.C. arrogantly strolling through the first-level corridors within the Stick, creating a ruckus. These ginormous 'Skin fans, dressed in loud women's XXXL-sized loud polka-dotted dresses and pink plastic pig snouts, wigs, fat beads, and other hog accessories, they loved the fact that every year Washington had the largest players on both lines of scrimmage, such as Dave Butz. The 49er Faithful razzed them heartily. But so far so good— all in good fun thus far. A conscientious security guard would be wise to monitor that activity, which may change in a heartbeat, but not me. I cruised on.

My heart pumped like a runaway locomotive while running up the final concrete corridor toward my press box assignment, totally psyched, listening to Bob Sarlatte's pregame announcements echoing over the PA system. His voice crackled through the same cheap stadium PA speakers the Beatles sang through during their final concert ever, August 29, 1966, right here at the Stick fifteen years ago already. Time certainly flies on by.

Some ladies on the second-level created a stir. There were shouts for security. The women invaded the men's room rather than stand in their eternal lines outside the lady's room. "Security, help!" someone yelled, repeating it. I wanted no part of that scene. How could that end well? Plus, it wasn't the kind of cry for help that held gravitas.

Thinking of the Beatles, knowing the words to every one of their songs and hearing someone shouting for help, I remember they performed "Help!" that night. I started singing to myself as I often did. "Won't you please, please help me, help me." Suddenly I heard *BA-BOOM!*

A shotgun blast. The revolution had begun. Sor

Someone below was shouting, "Help! Help!" And the Beatles.

"Everybody DOWN!" I screamed full throt concession stand line. The fans around me hit t in the air. Beers splashed into each other's faces. Hot dogs escaped their steamed, mustard-leathered buns.

We lay there in the slop on a cold concrete floor on a Monday night, wondering what to do next. The spilled beer and soda flowed down the ramp from above, covering us in grossness. Who was shooting? Who was shouting? It became eerily quiet.

I heard feet *tack-tack-tacking* on the concrete. I looked up toward, the sudden sound of a walkie-talkie sizzling. An SFPD officer stopped. He spotted me because of my damn uniform. The officer brayed, "Get up! Follow me!"

I started to say I didn't *do* anything or I'm not that kind of guard, but everyone stared at me. Off the two of us raced. We helped the SF Police Department in any way we could. But they never asked us to run into the stream of fire. I wish I had packed some heat, but I had no heat to pack.

Racing after him, my poor heart still pumping, *already* juiced on adrenaline, we ran down the exact same ramp I just ran up. I kept shouting at the bourgeois to get the hell out of our way until the cop shot me a look probably because no one was actually in the way.

His walkie-talkie crackled like a barking dog. Why are we heading into the line of fire? We sprinted out the back gate and immediately skidded to a stop. A small crowd had gathered around a green metal garbage dumpster seemingly built right into the outer Candlestick wall, the same damn dumpster I had those Hefty bags thrown away into when cleaning out the War Room's files many moons ago.

The cop talked into the handheld he shoved deeply into his face. He suddenly looked up toward the sky. I followed suit. We spotted a group of fans way up there peering down at us, over the wall, backlit, up in the absolute highest part of Candlestick Park, behind the nosebleed seats. I've been up there. It's like the Arctic. The fans wore parkas up

...nd, I think, built fires in the stands to stay warm. They were a ...erent breed. Nobody bothered these descendants of nomads.

Returning my vision to the task at hand, I burrowed my way through the growing crowd. "Excuse me. Excuse me." What were they looking at just outside the gate? I finally made it to the front of the small group gathered around a dumpster. When I looked into it, I was gobsmacked.

The lighting was poor. But I could make out a bearded fan in a green army/navy surplus jacket, 49ers wool hat, those green wool gloves with the fingers sticking out, who had to have been drunk. He looked so . . . peaceful. He must have fallen all the way from the tippy top of the stadium. He'd descended from the concrete back ramp where those Eskimos above looked down. Sitting on that wall, he had fallen over backward, maybe 150 feet. He crashed into this empty green metal dumpster. That was the source of the thunderous *boom* gun like sound we heard. Too bad the open dumpster had been empty. Trash may have provided a cushion.

I looked back up. Must've been an accident. However, if he was pushed, then it was murder!

The cop fiddled with his crackling walkie-talkie, shook the device, then his head, then my shoulder. "Lieutenant, run and notify Burns Security."

"Aye, aye, sir."

As I hauled ass back into the stadium, back up that same damn ramp again for the third time—man, this was getting tedious—the medevacs poured past me. I paused, spun around, and saw them hauling the fan's body away. He was out cold. Damnation! I felt bad for the fan. One mistake . . . well . . . hopefully, just unconscious, but also . . . do not think about it. Run.

Barging into El Capitán's office, sweating and panting, I grabbed a moment to compose myself and struggled to catch my breath. However, I could already tell from his smugness. The fascist already knew what had happened.

I began my report. He held a stop sign hand out. "No need to worry about it. Everything's covered," he said, flicking the air with his hand.

"Was the guy dead?" I asked a little scared.

"What guy?"

Incredulously, I screamed at the top of my lungs, "The man in the dumpster for Chrissakes!"

"No one knows nuthin' about nuthin'," he said and calmly ordered me to get back to work. That was his line, his mantra, for weeks afterward as well.

To this day, not a one of us grunts learned if he was dead or alive. You could never get a straight answer for *weeks* after his fall. Not a word in the papers or on the radio. That evening, I checked the local news on TV. Nothing. I'll never know.

My takeaway, however, was this: that fan still clutched his bottle of beer even after the great fall. That had to have stood for something, right? What a true fan. Such loyalty to the golden brew. I hope he survived, but well, like I said, best not to think about it.

I also lost my coveted assignment to guard the main press box that night and to bring the celebrity in for the halftime show, which all indications led to Joe Namath. El Capitán reassigned another guard to the juicy assignment since I was detained. That was a drag. Apparently, I had sauntered down to guard the bench where I told nary a soul of what just occurred. The game was already in progress. The unwritten rule at the bench was you can discuss the game but little else. So, after an unusually long head shake from this major distraction, I checked back in on the Great White Niner spirit I witnessed earlier.

CHAPTER 23

'88: THE GREAT WHITE SPIRIT

FORTUNATELY, SAN FRANCISCO'S boys were playing rather well. This *had* become such a tight team. Originally split in half, the team was seized by the reins and commanded by Montana, but Young got in a lot. The team also united over this common denominator: they were all under the rule of a new tyrant, Coach Walsh. He had previously kept players at arm's length. Tonight, he brought them back in and released the Great White Spirit.

The one thing any true fan will tell you was this: the very *best* thing about being a sports junkie was when you see and feel *true* team spirit. It's when the players perform greater than the sum of its parts. Every NFL player, when asked after they retire what they miss most, was exactly this, the team spirit, just being in the locker room with the guys when things were going well.

Being on a true *team was* magical. When you experience this team spirit, the good ol' college school spirit, or as the French say, *esprit de corps,* it was something you'd never rever forget. "Playing as a team" may be a tired cliché, but it's rarer than most folk realize. Hell, even way down at my lowly level, I felt it. The first summer I moved to California in fact. After setting up my stereo system, the very first thing I did whenever I moved into new surroundings, I would next look to join a baseball team. I was on a baseball team every summer I can remember and figured what better way was there to make new friends.

I tried joining the local Sunnyvale league only to discover disappointment upon learning they filled all the positions. I went on a waiting list. Eventually and luckily, there was enough on this list to form the final team in the league. Thus, a renegade team was born. Nobody knew anyone else beforehand. We were all starting off at the lowest common denominator, not being on a traditional formed team.

However, this united us. Amazingly, we found true team spirit and went undefeated, beating teams established for decades with tight cliques, budgets, and fan bases, none of which we had. Our uniforms resembled the Penn State football team's away uniforms, as bland and basic as white athletic socks. We even qualified for regionals and won the championship over superior teams. We made quite a name for ourselves throughout the regionals.

The local press picked up on our rags-to-riches story. We played popular exhibition games after the season, like against one of the nation's first all-female teams, the San Jose Rainbow. We won 5–3 but kind of cheated, bringing in the outfielders practically to play the infield because of their lack of power. However, we respected their greatness, especially on defense as they effortlessly turned two multiple times.

We even played a televised game against a nationally famous four-man team with a show-off pitcher named Eddie Feigner, called the King and his Court. All they had was a pitcher, catcher, first baseman, and a shortstop. We not only experienced our very first loss, but Eddie also threw a no-hitter and humiliated us with fancy pitches. I cringed watching the highlights on the evening news.

Of course, the following year, success went to the head of our well-fed coach, John, after his fifteen minutes of Warholian fame. I'll never forget some stud sitting on the end of the bench lacing up white spikes (we all wore black) on our first game of the second season. Dude even had his very own baseball bat inside his personalized bag. Of course, the rest of us shared the team bats.

"Who the hell is that?" I asked the guy who *used* to play third.

Found out Coach John brought in a bunch of ringers, guys who were stars on other teams. They rarely spoke to us grunts, never came to the postgame pizza-and-beer fetes, which had become our custom. These stars utterly destroyed the team chemistry, and we floundered. Nothing spoils success like success.

Nevertheless, experiencing that true team spirit the year-earlier remains one of my most cherished memories to this day. My heart, filled with gratitude, still soars like a hawk whenever I'm looking at my trophy.

But I digress. Back to the Niners game. The score was close in the second period, 10–7, when another cherished forever Forty-Niner moment arrived and added to the growing 49er lore.

Washington punted. John Taylor made a huge mistake. He fielded the punt at our own five-yard line. He should have let it bounce into the end zone for a touchback. Then he made a second mistake—running back to avoid the coverage. If he got tackled back there, it's either a safety or gives the 'Skins phenomenal field position. John Taylor set both the MNF record—which stands to this day—*and* the 49er franchise record by returning that punt ninety-five yards to pay dirt. More importantly, it gave SF the mojo, the momentum and turned the game around.

Psyched to the max, SF jumped out to a 23–7 halftime lead and never looked back. Joe Cool had a hand in all three first-half touchdowns. The Niners allowed Washington a merciful garbage TD at the end of the game with the score 37–14. The spirited team of Forty-Niners thus crucified the defending Super Bowl champion Washington Redskins 37–21.

Next, San Francisco went on a tear and won the Western Division yet again. Guess who they drew in the first round of their 1988 playoff appearance? You guessed it. The Minnesota Vikings. Same team who created the 9ers downward spiral. And man, were the Vikes ever cocky. They said they'd prove last year was no fluke.

Pregame, we relaxed in our usual seats inside our crusty War Room. Our intellectual discussion centered on none other than Joe Montana[33] who finished the regular season stronger than ever.

---

33   The Comeback Kid won a National Championship at Notre Dame (1977). He then starred for sixteen seasons in the NFL. Joe Cool earned four Super Bowl Rings, became the first three-time Super Bowl MVP, currently holds records for most SB career passes without a single interception and the highest QB rating of 127.8. Joe earned two NFL MVP awards and joined the Hall of Fame his first year of eligibility. In 2006, *Sports Illustrated* named him the number 1 clutch quarterback of all time.

I said, "To paraphrase Mark Twain, the rumors of Joe's death were greatly exaggerated."

Gunner spit the beyond-gross fluid into a 7-Up bottle, shoved more tobacco into his chipmunk cheek, and replied, "When he's done, he'll easily have the record for most comeback victories of all time."

"Yeah," I added another sugar packet to the black sludge inside my white Styrofoam cup, hoping to lessen that bitter bite. "No matter how much the Niners are down in the fourth, with Joe back there, everyone knows he'll find a way to win the damn game every time."

Gunner said, "I think it's 'cos he has such amazing vision."

"Whatd'ya mean?"

"Most NFL-caliber QBs can look for a secondary receiver if their primary target's covered, right? Joe Cool looks for all four receivers, man. Dude knows where they are on each and every play. But what do you think? You've managed to brownnose your way onto the field. You're the closest to him."

Gunner was referring to earlier while Joe warmed up and my photographer friend let me snap a shot of him after R. C. yelled, "C'mon, Montana, smile once in a while."

Gunner's never going to let that go. "I'm glad you asked, you jealous little prick. I actually have a strong opinion as to why he's by far the greatest athlete in all of sports, second only to Babe Ruth who was light-years above his competition at the time. Definitely the best *quarterback* ever. I've watched him play for, what, eight years now? And my answer is . . . drum roll please."

Gunner and Brad played along— taking it too far as always— pounding the cheap veneer tabletop, completely spilling the lava from our table onto the floor.

I smiled. "It's because Joe has eyes in the back of his head. Other quarterbacks get sacked all the time from their blind side. Never Joe. I can't figure out how he does it. How he always knows. Just when he's about to get sacked from behind, *boom*, he instinctively takes off. Joe knows. Instead of a ten-yard loss, he has this visceral sense and sprints downfield for a first down or scrambles and hits Rice or Clark for a big gainer. That's why he's the greatest."[34]

Brad was nursing a major hangover judging by the hat pulled over his completely bloodshot eyes and his feet up on the table. Brad always said, "It's essential to blow the pipes out at least once a week." Guess that day was yesterday.

He chimed in, "I think it's 'cos of where he's from, pure and simple."

Gunner and I, waiting for the rest of his theory as he stared at his Mickey Mouse watch, asked in unison, "And?"

"Oh sorry. Think about it. Look at all the talent that came from that cradle in western Pennsylvania. The best quarterbacks of all time from that same clump of ground: the former comeback king, Johnny Unitas. Also, Dan Marino and Joe Namath."

"George Blanda, Jim Kelly, and Terry Hanratty," Gunner added.

I tossed in, "Mike Ditka and Tony Dorsett, but let's stick with just the quarterbacks. Don't forget Heisman Trophy winner Johnny Lujack,

---

34   In 1999, Time Inc./*Sports Illustrated* put out the Special Collector's edition: *Greatest Athletes of the 20th Century* (authors Tim Crothers and John Garrity. ISBN – 892129-18-3, prepared by Bishop Books, Inc). The book lists the twenty-five greatest athletes highlighting Babe Ruth, Michael Jordan, and Wayne Gretzsky. But for their cover, they chose Joe Montana.

Babe Parilli, and what about Penn State's All-American QB Chuck Fusina? The list is long. But what are you sayin', Joe's great just 'cos he comes from western PA?"

"I don't know, but something's going on out there. Maybe they oughta study it. Maybe something in the water."

Gunner said, "Or maybe it's because they work harder growing up in that blue-collar steel community, knowin' sports may be the only way out of a career inside a hot-as-hell steel plant."

Suddenly, my sideline partner, R. C. Owens stuck his prominent head into our room. "You boys wanna see sumthin' you never seen before? I'd suggest getting your lazy white asses downstairs fast. Team meetin'. Hurry or you be missin' it."

We looked at each other. R. C. never does that. Gunner whipped out the flask as per tradition. We three gulped, gagged, wiped the tears away, then sprinted to where we knew the team met and—obviously harrumph—needed an extra layer of security.

Wow. You had to appreciate how incredibly shy the person we were talking about was. I know for a fact from guarding him. Like the American Indian warriors of old, this man led by action, not words. Yet there he was, in front of the entire team using words. The audience was riveted. Some seated, some standing, but all hanging on to every word. It was a total *surprise.* Joe Montana, Joe Cool himself, led the pregame pep talk. He spoke gallantly while his mentor, Coach Walsh, stood in the background like a proud papa, arms crossed, grinning like a Cheshire cat, watching his finest work perform.

Joe pointed a football at his teammates, exhorting them not to take *any*thing for granted this time around. The younger players were getting psyched, hyperventilating. This was special. The veterans like Randy Cross and Bubba Paris smiled broadly. They knew. This was another forever Forty-Niner moment. Shy Joe never spoke out like this. If he did, I never saw it. Joe ended his pregame speech with one of football's most hallowed passages, the traditional, the one, the only, "Now let's get out there and KICK SOME EFFIN ASS!"

This time, there was no sneaking up on anybody, no overconfidence exuding from Niner pores. They had learned their lesson from experience the best of teachers and not from Walsh's warnings. "One thorn of experience is worth a whole wilderness of warning."[35] After waiting an entire year, the 49ers extracted their vengeance, pulverizing the Vikings 34–9 as they should have done last year.

Off San Francisco marched into the NFC Championship game against, once again, the heavily favored Bears from the fine city of Chicago. Once again, Da Bears gave our team plenty of motivational newspaper clippings for posting on the Niner bulletin boards: "The softer San Francisco team would *never* be able to compete in a game inside brutal Bear country, in minus 26 degrees weather with the wind chill factor at Soldier Field. No way.

"The finesse team from *Frisco* couldn't possibly grind it out with The Monsters of Midway on this day, in Bear weather, in Soldier Field," the local press wrote.

Some folk just never learn.

By the way, San Franciscans despise the insulting word *Frisco*. When I first moved there, the older generation scolded me whenever I used it, saying, "You mean *San Francisco*."

One of the biggest drags of living in *San Fran*cisco for fifteen years was every time I went to a national business convention where peers came from all over our great nation or whenever I went back home to Pennsylvania, or just when traveling with the team, I always had to answer for how openly *gay* SF supposedly was. The whole gay thing.

Whenever people came to visit, it was always, "Hey, Rick, where's all the gays?"

I'd reply, "If you really need to see them for whatever reason, there *is* a place I can take you. It's a former little Irish/Italian neighborhood and a mere six square blocks."

In 1978, the same year of my immigration to California, America's first gay supervisor, Harvey Milk, revitalized the neighborhood. You may recall he was later assassinated in city hall by a jealous Dan White.

---

35   James Russell Lowell, American poet.

Urban myth famously said Dan blamed his murderous behavior on his massive intake of Hostess Twinkies, thus the birth of the Twinkie Defense.

I'd say, "If need be, we can cruise into the Castro District, where they live and work." Their vision was always of an entire city covered with gays crawling through the windows. They'd find that was simply not the case. Like when my wife's oldest brother and my good friend Danny Holcomb would visit from the deep South with his son, Danny, I would ask, "Where you wanna go?"

It was always, "Let's go fand'us summa dem dare quares agin, Reck, like las'tam."

And off we'd go, driving around the Castro District. It'd be, "Look ovah deya, there's a coupla a dem dare quares pressed up aginst dat dare tree."

Also, two friends of mine, every Halloween, would come out and take a gazillion photos of the unparalleled Castro District Annual Halloween parade then show them to everyone. They loved the pregnant nuns the best.

The Castro District was—is—amazing. Best theater around, the iconic Castro Theatre, built in 1922 with its Wurlitzer organ performance before each show, great restaurants, wonderful pizza shops like Marcello's, and a few damn good bars for both straights and gays alike. The Castro was clean, safe, the inhabitants friendly, and because they are wealthy—two breadwinners, no kids—the upkeep was of high quality throughout. They are well educated, and by voting as a solid block in unison with the hippie Haight-Ashbury District next door, they got the constant attention of anyone running for office, whether Mayor Feinstein, Mayor Brown, or Mayor Gavin.

The point was this: it's just one impressive district, one patch among many creating the San Francisco quilt, and not the whole damn city.

Anyway, back to the game. And as Yogi Berra said, "It looked like déjà vu all over again."

San Francisco once again ran roughshod over the Bears *in* Soldier Field, *in* Bear weather, *in* Bear country and battered them with yet another *phys*ical beating: San Francisco 28, Chicago 3.

Coach Walsh took great delight in these massacres because he hated the labels the Chi-Town news outlets kept trying to hang on his team to no avail. Once again, I proudly donned my bright golden Niners jacket to all my business conventions.

Since the game was on the road, I checked it out on TV. As a married man now, I watched this rout with my gorgeous, new wife, Maureen. Coincidentally, she got her nursing degree in Bear country, Augustana School of Nursing near Lake Michigan in downtown Chicago. We watched in an outdoor bar in Hawaii with only three walls—the missing wall overlooked the Pacific Ocean. Stunning place and I wish I remembered the name. However, I made damn sure to get an assignment for Super Bowl XXIII against—once again—the Cincinnati Bengals, who were riding high at 12–4.

It was significantly better to watch football now after years of observing with the big-time spectators like my dad who had an uncanny ability to predict the next play, Bill Walsh Sr., and hearing Madden and Sumerall talking smack about the game both on and especially off the mike.

But who cared? It was back to the Super Bowl.

CHAPTER 24

SUPER BOWL XXIII, JANUARY 22, 1989

Joe Robbie Stadium, Miami

H OORAY! BACK TO the Super Bowl after four long years. Tons of Bengal fans made a racket but the 49er Faithful also arrived in spirited droves.

I schlepped into my traditional spot and walked out a little before the game in front of our bench. My uniform showed people looking at me that I was a lieutenant. They asked questions, figuring that I'm all experienced and such. The truth was I knew about as much of what I was supposed to be doing than I did back in '81 when I started, which wasn't much.

I gazed toward the crowd. Okay, no one running toward the bench I'm protecting. Maybe the fans think I'd take a bullet for Coach Walsh. That's about as likely as NATO inviting the Soviet Union to join their club.

Unlike the last Niner Super Bowl in our backyard at Stanford, practically a home game since Burns Security ran things, there would be no locker room door watching here. Instead, I was assigned to guard both Billy Joel who'd soon sing our national anthem and his drop-dead gorgeous wife, Christie Brinkley, during their joint interview. Everyone just had to pass that way on their way to somewhere to check the super couple out. I heard every excuse known to man as to why they just had to pass that way. Everyone asked me for some scoops on them, but truth be told, they were both grateful to be there. Celebrities are always appreciative and well behaved at Super Bowls because of the enormity of the spectacle. Billie nailed the national anthem using no bells, no whistles, just a man and a mike. Christie possessed that gorgeous girl-next-door look and an approachable persona. Afterward, unnoticed, I headed back to guard the ol' bench—surprised by how strong the breeze had become.

Weird. This was the friggin' Super Bowl, but it felt like any old game. I talked awhile to an equipment manager who just came out from the locker room. Coach Walsh once again was taking his nap up by the whiteboard, and everyone had to be quiet and walk around him. There was an odd theatricality about that man, but it got everyone relaxed.

I was certainly relaxed. Bored. I walked onto the field in front of our bench and mindlessly kicked at the turf like a little kid. A giant divot flew up. Shit. A couple of game managers getting the water and gear ready near the bench shot me the look. Embarrassed, I smiled and replaced it best I could. However, feeling the turf between my fingers, I noted the field was in god-awful shape. Later, in just the first quarter alone, two players snapped their legs on this terrible turf.

We lost stud offensive tackle, and Joe's protection of his blind side left tackle Steve Wallace[36] a mere three plays into the game to a broken ankle. The Bengals Tim Krumrie broke his leg in two places, his tibia, and his fibula, nine plays later. Both men left the field on stretchers. Boy, you spend your life dreaming of playing in the big one, and just as the game gets underway, next thing you know, they're hauling you off on a stretcher with your career in jeopardy (although both men came back).

The other players, horrified by this brutality, adjusted but bitched about the playing surface all game. You'd think for the Super Bowl they'd find a way to prevent a sloppy field.

Speaking of sloppy, that's how the game started. Neither offense could get going. The defenses dominated. The main reason the Niners could not get untracked was Sam Wyche. This former disciple of Coach Walsh, his former assistant, and his former quarterback's coach, helped Bill Walsh find and recruit the legendary Joe Montana. He knew Joe only too well and came up with a brilliant game plan to take away Joe's short passing schemes and clog up his running lanes. He knew our offense intimately since he was once part of the brain trust that formed it. Thus, Sam was the man with the plan and created a solid defensive scheme to stop Joe and Coach Bill Walsh's West Coast Offense in its tracks.

The 49ers entered this tilt with the worst record entering a Super Bowl in history at 10–6. Cincy, on the other hand, had the number 1 offense in the NFL, invented running a no-huddle offense for an entire game rather than just the two-minute drill, and took the league by storm. Their All-Pro quarterback, Boomer Esiason, was the overwhelming league MVP. He had the Bengals rolling and indestructible. Don't forget. There was also a little-added motivation: that little thing called *revenge* on their side as well. Their lustful thirst for vengeance evolved from their last Super Bowl appearance when they almost defeated the

---

36   Steve Wallace was no mere left tackle protecting Joe's blind side. Besides owning three Super Bowl rings from the Niners, he is credited with revolutionizing the left tackle position mainly for his one-on-one techniques taking on the game's leading pass rushers.

49ers, but thanks to the famous San Francisco goal line stand, Cincy came up short.

Secondly, last year, the second game of the regular season, leading San Francisco 26–20, Sam Wyche's Bengals had possession of the ball in the final minute. They simply needed to run out the clock. Miraculously, somehow, they screwed up. They blew it. They left two whole seconds on the clock.

They felt it didn't matter, however. Mississippi one, Mississippi two, game over. Right? Wrong. They left the 49ers time to run one final desperate play. They all knew Montana would try to hit Rice as time expired, so they simply covered him tighter than white on rice, pun intended. It mattered not. Joe, Jerry, and two seconds on the clock were like a gin, a tonic, and two limes during the summer at the pool. They combined for the magical Hail Mary game-ending touchdown pass—another forever Forty-Niner moment—giving San Francisco a stunning 27–26 victory.

But that was then. This was now. Super Bowl XXIII was all Cincinnati all game thus far. The Sam Wyche–led Bengals were avenging those painful losses. Coach Wyche, I remember watching him standing right next to Coach Walsh during the 1981 Super Bowl victory season, was one step ahead of the Genius thus far. Sam knew Joe's tendencies only too well and was killing the West Coast Offense. Coach Walsh tried hiding the Niner formations, but Sam recognized them and sent in defensive audibles.

Coach Walsh, in a way, was coaching against a younger, hungrier version of himself. Yet San Francisco, though playing poorly on offense and on the ropes, somehow hung in there—mainly on the strength and chutzpah of their defensive unit coached masterfully by George Seifert, the most underrated coach in the NFL.

Halftime came with the score tied 3–3. Nobody in their wildest dreams thought at this point that a 3–3 snore fest would turn into one of the most exciting games ever in the Super Bowl annals of time.

Regardless, now, it was halftime, a break from football. The time had come for—the one, the only—*Elvis Presto*! Thus, began the most bizarre halftime show of all time. A bad Elvis impersonator named

Elvis Presto performed, not even *trying* to hide his lip-synching, which I kind of appreciated. I hate lip-synching to death. Sing or don't sing. But Elvis performed only one Elvis song. The remainders were from *Grease*, Mitch Ryder, or the Stray Cats for some odd reason. Why do Elvis songs when you're an Elvis impersonator, right?

It was the first ever halftime show in 3D. I assumed the bizarre behavior was supposed to look good in 3D on TV, but if you were live at the game, with no 3D glasses, it was just plain weird. A collection of heads shook side to side when the strange spectacle mercifully ended.

The second half got underway. San Francisco set a goal at halftime R. C. told us: stop Icky Woods, the Bengal's star running back. Icky had already rushed for sixty yards in just the first thirty minutes of the game. He fired up the Bengal crowd as well, doing the Icky Shuffle whenever he gained yet another key first down. The Icky Shuffle further fired up the Bengal fans when he performed it on the sidelines. The coaches in the San Fran halftime locker room asked team captain Ronnie Lott if he would eradicate this problem. He said he'd take care of it.

Ronnie Lott hammered Icky to start the half. I mean, he put a hit on Icky like a meteor striking a rogue planet. Icky stumbled around, seeing little stars flying around his head. After the hit, Icky, now rubber legged, stumbled less than twenty yards the remainder of the game. Icky, now sicky, was no longer so tricky, a nonfactor. No more shuffles. Every Niner on the bench took note. Ronnie, the hardest-hitting defensive halfback of all time, did it again.

The Niners kept the game close with a big play here or there and, somehow despite being thoroughly outplayed, were only behind 16–13 with 3:20 left on the clock. The contest had been a defensive struggle throughout. The Bengals had just taken the lead on a field goal and had momentum firmly planted on their side.

The 49ers returned the ensuing kickoff to their own measly fifteen-yard line with 3:10 remaining in the Super Bowl. However, an illegal blocking penalty on the play pushed the ball back. The referee gave us the bad news saying, "Half the distance to the goal line."

The potential scape-goat jogged off the field after the loud proclamation of his sin was announced for incurring the potential game-ending penalty. I'll be kind and not mention him here. I noticed he entered the extreme opposite end of the bench, avoiding the laser penetrating gaze of Coach Walsh. I walked down to guard him a little bit in case some crazed fan attacked although that never happened once in my career. I had to do something.

The Cincy crowd, heavily concentrated down in our part of the end zone, went bonkers after the back-killing penalty. We watched in horror as the ref, goose-stepping like a Nazi storm trooper, marched the ball back to the eight-yard line, a ridiculous ninety-two yards away from paydirt.

The Bengals smelled blood. What a crucial, costly penalty, adding significant momentum to their side.

The Bengal D huddled on the sidelines, knowing if they forced a three and out, got the ball in good field position, ran the clock out, the Super Bowl was all theirs, all theirs. Bru ha ha.

I heard later that future *Monday Night Football* commentator Chris Collingsworth, then a star receiver for the Bengals, screamed at his players at the top of his lungs to stop celebrating.

"Don't you realize who they have over there at quarterback? You guys crazy? They can still win!"

Nevertheless, the Bengal defense sauntered out onto the field with a prominent swagger, moving their beefy arms upward, extolling the Cincy crowd into pandemonium. Like victorious gladiators, the game was theirs for the taking. No team in Super Bowl history ever ended a game with a game-winning drive. That was for Hollywood or the regular season. That doesn't happen in the Super Bowl.

Their captain told his teammates on the field, "Lissen' up, guys. The Niners beat us the last time we met in the Super Bowl. But there ain't no way in hell these guys are driving ninety-two yards against us this time. No. Way."

Their defense yelled back. "No way."

The clock slipped below the three-minute mark, each valuable second ticking off the board. Or to lightly paraphrase Raymond

Chandler from his book *The Lady in the Lake*, "The *seconds* went by on tiptoe, with their fingers to their lips."

In *this* book, however, it appeared to be the final chapter of any further Forty-Niner folk talk. Montana met with his mentor, Coach Walsh. The two legends liked to kneel in the grass together, away from the others. It always looked to me like Coach was drawing the play in the dirt with his finger saying, "This guy goes that way, that guy goes this way, and you do this."

Recollected was the calm demeanor between the two greats while their offense waited on the field. I looked up into the stands. People screaming as loud as humanly possible. I watched Joe and his coach, capturing the moment. There they were—the Silver Fox and Joe Cool chatting amiably during an impossibly long television timeout on the sidelines five yards away from me. John Updike in his phenomenal *Run Rabbit Run* book wrote, "Moments, stolen from time, are compressed as diamonds."

This was one of those moments, as rich as the hardest of diamonds. Joe Robbie Stadium rocked. The entire place physically shook. I planned on following the ball, keeping imaginary people from rushing the field in my classic security guard stance one final time.

However, this time, as a spectator, after watching games with my dad, with Bill Walsh Sr., and with R. C. Owens, I realized my transformation from simply watching the action to *seeing* the big picture took a while because I can be a notoriously slow learner. But once I finally get it right, I get it for life. I watched the coaches for their strategy. I watched the Niner huddle. I was later told in the postgame locker room interviews that *two* of the offensive linemen were hyperventilating. Others said they were just plain scared. Scared they would, quote, "commit the big fifteen-yard penalty that costs us the game" and then a lifetime of infamy.

Others just plain worried they would not be able to *hear* the audibles Joe barked out at the line of scrimmage. Joe's voice was extremely hoarse, nearly gone, hanging by a thread. Big problem, that.

Being an offensive lineman in this situation was almost too intense. You needed that quick jump to position yourself to stop the charging adrenaline-filled, lightning-quick defensive lineman. If the guy you're assigned to sacks the QB, you be the scape-goat.

If you jump a split-second too soon, you're offsides. What if your team scores on that play but your penalty negates the winning score? It could mean both the game and your surname go down in history as the culprit. The ref shouts out your jersey number over the PA system. The camera zooms in for a close up of your face to the national viewing audience. If you missed the audible and Joe's voice currently reduced to a loud whisper, you would not even know what the play was. Moreover, as the climax approached with history writing itself, no one heard a damn thing beyond the incessant roar.

I'll always remember watching ol' number 16 jogging out toward that huddle, with that unique stride he had. Shudders. Chills. This was it. But my god, he was ninety-two yards away with no voice and veiled in pure bedlam.

First, you will hear my eyewitness account culled from my postgame notes, immediately followed by how it actually went down.

Joe called for the huddle—which was a chaotic mess. Too many nervous linemen were talking at the same time, freaking out. Others inside the extra-tight circle shouted, "Shut up! Be quiet! Let's hear what Joe says!"

Then, inexplicably, the comic book Hollywood *compressed moment* arrived right on time.

Joe bent into the huddle. The players first looked toward the end zone, their goal, as was custom, ninety-two long yards away. They looked at the clock, 3:10 remaining. Then bent into the huddle. But Joe popped his head back up, looking out at a section within the 70,000-odd crowd behind me. He then stuck his head back into the huddle.

Next, two other heads popped up. They quickly went back down. With everyone's heartbeats accelerating, the Montana helmet popped up yet again followed by ten other golden helmets, all looking in the same direction up into the crowd. Then they all went back down like so many cartoon ostriches burying their heads. Joe called the play. I kept looking behind me as did others around me.

"What in the hell were they looking at? Why now?" I asked aloud.

My glances were quick glances. So strong was my fear of the fascists or one of those "too into it" full-time supervisor guards discovering me and waving for me to come *do* something.

Those guys always stirred up their own trouble. Although at this junction, perfectly positioned on the sidelines, they'd have to drag me off the field kicking and screaming. I wasn't moving. Not now. This was history in the making or disappointment to the max. But wait . . . what was happening?

It was a remarkable thing to see. Goofy even. I looked along the sidelines. What was I missing? The players and coaches exchanged sideward glances, throwing their hands up in the air. No one knew what the heck they were *doing* out there in that huddle—at such a crazy time no less.

Not until the story broke much later did we finally learn what had happened. Joe had cemented his reputation as *Joe Cool.*

He calmly slid into that intensely packed huddle, where everyone nervously chattered. Everyone listened for the play. Joe said something, which didn't sound like the play. Joe repeated himself. Living in the moment, slowing the intensity down as he always did in big-game situations. He was, in fact, not even calling the play.

"There, right there, in the stands, standing near the exit ramp," Montana said to the hyperventilating, massive tackle Harris Barton, "isn't that John Candy?"

He and Harris had a longtime thing going about spotting celebrities in the crowd from the field, but that was during the regular season. But right now? Surrounded by gravitas thicker than the brown gravy our mothers once poured over our mashed potatoes.

Harris popped up then back down and, shaking his head, giggling nervously, answered, "Yeah, it is. It's him all right."

The other ten heads popped up following Joe's. They all spotted John Candy and dropped back down. By golly, Joe was right. Standing near the exit ramp *was* John Candy—the funniest comedian around in 1988 and 1989. The big guy enjoying himself at the big game, big time. I chuckled. Just looking at that round guy made you laugh. The Niner offense had solid fat smiles spread across their faces in the huddle and calmed down. Some laughed heartily. Others giggled like school kids. One even exclaimed, "Fucking Joe Montana, right? Of course, we can do this. What in God's name are we worrying about?"

Joe had removed them from the game just for a *moment*. But sometimes, that's all it takes.

"Play ball!" screamed a zebra. Montana snapped to, officially called the play, then yelled, "Ready?"

"BREAK!" the team responded along with the perfectly timed hand clap. Mamma Mia. Joe had altered the mood.

The strategy *chess match* was *on*. The battle of wits between the silver fox Bill Walsh versus his former wise pupil Sam Wyche began. Thus far, young grasshoppa was calling his best game ever. However, this was crunch time, do or die. No one outwits Coach Walsh during crunch time. No one.

Coach Wyche guarded the sidelines like a junkyard dog. San Francisco receivers would not be making that sideline catch, putting their two dainty feet down and skipping out of bounds to stop the clock, Coach Wyche reckoned. Surely, that's what they were planning. He'd seen it before.

He must've thought further; *Does Coach Walsh not realize I studied Joe's famous two-minute drills for two weeks straight after the season ended in preparation for just this moment in time on the world's largest stage? Does he not know we spent hours upon hours at practice defending exactly for this—the upcoming two-minute drill?*

We are positively prepared to prevent any magical Montana moments. No game-ending drives. Doesn't Walsh remember it was me, Coach Wyche, who was Joe's quarterback coach? It was I who worked with Joe closely on these same drives and thus stand supremely confident, more than any other man on the planet—to stop him, he must've thought.

Rather than force the issue, as most coaches would, Coach Walsh had Montana first dump a pair of completions smack dab into the middle of the field, inbounds, one to Roger Craig and one to tight end John Frank—exactly where no one expected. You never throw over the middle since that chews up the clock. But Walsh and Joe did exactly that.

Joe's next pass went seven yards on a quick curl-out to Rice.

Damn him. Coach Wyche countered. Those seven-yarders won't beat us. He's going back over the middle for big chunks of yardage. Wyche feigned guarding the sidelines, but *after* his center snapped the ball, he sent his linebackers to cover that suddenly vulnerable middle of the field.

Bill Walsh was one step ahead. Instead, Bill crazily ordered a pair of time-consuming runs, the West Coast–style long handoffs, meaning Joe drops back to pass but suddenly hands it off to his blocking back, Roger Craig way later than a standard draw play. It worked. Roger Craig fired straight up the gut to reach their own thirty-five-yard line and pick up a valuable first down. The holes were right where the Bengal linebackers normally would have been had they not dropped back to guard the middle for more short passes.

So back to the line of scrimmage, or as they say, back into the box went the Bengal linebackers to shut this sudden running game down. Wyche probably thought, *They're not running on us.*

Next play: Montana, running his patented two-minute no-huddle offense, quickly dropped back exactly seven steps, crow-hopped forward two steps, and confidently fired a strike between two defenders, completing a seventeen-yard pass to Rice racing across the field. It sailed right over the Bengal linebackers' heads in the spot on the field the linebackers just vacated. Beautiful. Jerry gracefully slipped out of bounds and hustled back to the line of scrimmage. Joe had advanced his team to the Bengals forty-eight-yard line. The drive was on.

The problem was these long developing plays were taking too much time off the board. The clock slipped below two minutes. Wyche decided Walsh and Montana would abandon the run, so instead, he dropped his linebackers back deep into pure pass coverage.

To counter, Joe had his running backs quickly sprint out of the backfield into the middle of the field—again where the linebackers normally roamed but were now back too far in their pass defense. Joe fired a thirteen-yard completion to Craig to move to the Bengal thirty-five-yard line. The Niners were methodically on the move but gambling with the clock.

I stole a glance across our bench. The entire 49er sideline frantically waved their arms downfield, extolling the big linemen to hurry up, get to the line of scrimmage—time was running out. The poor big guys had to drop back seven yards in their pass protection pocket then hustle downfield thirteen yards for the next play, thus a twenty-yard sprint with no huddle in which to catch their breath. They were exhausted but dug deep and sprinted.

Montana, hyperventilating from running, passing, and screaming signals through a hoarse voice, signaled to Walsh to call a timeout and catch his breath, but Walsh frantically waved Joe downstream. Keep the Bengals on their heels. Joe needed a break. Maybe a little water to get his voice back.

I later learned, Coach never heard him, only saw him and just kept waving Joe forward, downfield. You can't imagine how loud it gets down on the field in these situations. Trust me, it's significantly louder than up in the stands. Being able to hear is such an intricate part of the game.

I looked across the field. The Bengal sidelines were pushing their hands up and down saying, "Slow them down. Stop their drive."

The intensity, so thick in the air it felt like an automotive airbag popped open and pushed against your face. *Remember to breathe,* I thought.

Wyche, crouching along the sideline, tugged on his cap and thought, "Gotta stop 'em right here, right now." He smiled, reached into his bag of tricks, and stuck six men on the line of scrimmage. They blitzed, and the assault collapsed the 49er pocket. He had struck back.

A hurried Montana, now only dropping back only three steps out of desperation to save time, threw his first incomplete pass of the drive, letting it sail out of bounds. He threw it away rather than take the sack—the one thing the Niners absolutely could not afford to take. They had no time to lose yardage in this manner nor a penalty, thus moving backward. Either one would kill the drive and allow the Bengals the opportunity to reclaim the momentum. However, that's exactly what happened.

Next play, center Randy Cross, of all people, committed an illegal man downfield penalty. The crippling penalty negated a much-needed successful pass play down the middle. The zebras moved the ball all the way back to the forty-five-yard line, bringing up *second down and twenty* to go with only 1:15 remaining in the game.

"Go for the interception," Wyche ordered his linebackers. "Now Montana has to pass. No other option. This is the play of the game. Right now. Pick it off over the middle. Win the first Super Bowl *ever* for Cincinnati. Play like champions out there."

The Niner momentum shattered like a Ford Pinto in an accident. Cincy had regained the big mo. They knew even if they did not intercept, one more incomplete pass would bring up a "third and twenty" situation, meaning the 9ers would be desperate.

Wyche had his linebackers line up close to the line, disguising their coverage, then dropped back over the middle and thus this time . . . catch the sly ol' fox Walsh off guard. *He throws over the middle just one more time, we intercept, we win the Super Bowl, and the glory is ours,* thought Wyche, I imagined.

Furthermore, since this was an obvious long-passing play, there'd be no more quick releases from Joe. He had to drop back seven steps, allowing his receivers time to get downfield. Thus, Cincy brought the house and ran a defensive stunt. It was a full-out pass rush resembling a jailbreak.

But Joe Cool had his mojo workin'. The greater the intensity, the more he slowed down his metabolism. He calmly dropped way back as if it were just a regular season game. The offensive line formed the perfect pocket, protected their fearless leader, and Joe Cool fired a perfect spiral toward—you guessed it—the middle of the field.

Surrounded by three defenders anticipating this, Jerry Rice appeared in the exact postage stamp spot where Joe had fired it, caught the pass in midstream, and sprinted downfield like a gazelle for a twenty-seven-yard completion. Rice caught the ball in stride at the thirty-three and evaded *three* Bengal defenders. He scurried all the way down to the eighteen-yard line before Cincinnati's Horton finally tackled him, thus preventing the touchdown. Joe was amazingly passing within that furious Bengal pass rush. It was Jerry Rice's single all-time best clutch play as a Forty-Niner up to that point.

Cincinnati was back on its heels, stunned. They had three defenders anticipating that pass. Walsh sent in the next play. The 9ers were crazily wide-eyed and breathing like steam locomotives. But to a man, they noted, Joe was completely relaxed, as calm as a country pond among the dew of the early morn. His demeanor relaxed everyone around him.

Next play, Joe dropped back, his killer instinct on display. He fired an eight-yard pass to Roger Craig—over the middle, unreal—during the chaos. That advanced San Francisco to the Bengal ten-yard line.

However, an obstacle loomed of great gravitas. Time was about to expire. This was it! Only thirty-nine quick ticks remained on the board.

"Don't panic!" I yelled to no one in particular. Like everyone around me, I cupped my hands and screamed like a banshee to release tension. Everyone around me, cheek to jowl, bellowed for the same reason, the noise so loud, it threatened to puncture your eardrums.

Montana calmly stepped up to the line of scrimmage and got under center like it was any other game. He tried barking out signals, but his voice was completely gone from screaming plays and audibles over the deafening crowd. The 49ers lined up and froze into their offensive positions. Beautiful. The golden helmets shined along the line of scrimmage. The Stick so loud it was as if you pressed your ear to an airplane engine.

However, a huge problem arose. R. C. Owens, wearing the official bright white Super Bowl cap, in his excitement directly in front of the left side of the bench, waving his overly long arms, yelled at his team, "Wrong formation! You're in the wrong formation!"

I looked and looked but could not tell. But Cincinnati, too, was barely holding on in all the bedlam. All the oxygen was sucked out of the air. The deafening sound even increased somehow as every coach and every fan just kept on screaming their bloody heads off. It was all so out of control, and everybody was frantic . . . except . . . one man—Joe Cool.

Montana, who had just strategically moved his team straight down the field with pinpoint passing and timely audibles, continued slowing the game down in his mind. He lived in the moment, completely relaxed, the Montana way. Joe set Jerry Rice into motion. Jerry, going from the right of the formation to the left, jogged behind Montana and the line of scrimmage. Very visible. Every eye —including mine— fixated on Jerry Rice, Joe's go-to receiver in the final clutch.

Immediately, two Bengals pulled out of their defensive alignments and smartly glided left-to-right to double-team Rice, mirroring his speed, like two hawks monitoring their prey. Sam Wyche called for the double team on Rice who had already corralled eleven passes for 215 yards and the Niners' only touchdown.

The center, Randy Cross snapped the ball.

Joe sent Craig out to run a pattern. Craig figured he was the primary receiver on this play. Even though he lined up incorrectly, he sprinted out for the pass. Our fullback, Tom Rathman, also mistakenly lined up—in Craig's position. He went out for the pass as well, since that *was* the position as per the called play. Thus, Joe's flanks were completely exposed. A simple blitz from an outside linebacker position would easily have nailed Joe or, at a minimum, disrupted the play.

I was surprised, seeing both running backs take off as receivers after the play initiated. They sprinted to the same spot in the end zone. No one stayed home to protect Joe from the Bengal blitz as was almost always the case. He'd have to get rid of the ball quickly. He was all alone back there. Intense!

John Taylor, the second option, hadn't caught a pass all day. Can't throw to a receiver who hadn't caught a pass all day. He might easily drop it from inactivity. Thus, every eye in the park glued firmly on Jerry Rice.

The Bengals charged the quarterback with all their might. Sack Joe. Game over. The magnificent Niner offensive line tried holding back the attack. The center, Randy Cross, not having his usual great game—he botched a long snap earlier that cost SF a field goal that would have been valuable right about now. He also was nearly the scape-goat because of his terrible penalty earlier on this drive.

Cross snapped the ball. No one was directly over him, so he looked left. The rush was contained on that side. He dropped back, further protecting Joe. He looked right and spotted the blitzing surge heading straight for Joe. He drove into what seemed like a human stream of water after the dam broke.

A desperate Bengal hand shoved under Randy's face mask. The Bengal frantically tried getting Randy the hell out of his way. He merely had to get to Joe and stop him from passing. He just had to get past this one last hurdle, Randy Cross, sack Joe, and win his lifetime dream—the Super Bowl.

Randy, his final play ever as a Forty-Niner, held on with all his might, his head pushed back to the max, as far as his thick neck allowed, giving Joe just enough time to look downfield.

Rice, having a career day, streaked to the corner of the end zone. The obvious target looked back for that pass with both defenders as close to him as pages in a book.

Everyone watched. Joe would pass far and high to Jerry. Let him go up after it. Joe set his feet, glanced over to Rice, and quickly fired a bullet as hard as he could throw it.

But wait! The pass did not sail to Rice. It did not.

Instead, Joe threw straight, hard, and true right down the extreme *middle* of the field—a perfect spiral like a dagger into the very heart of the Bengal defense—and into the able arms of the streaking John Taylor.

Joe finished the drive with a beautiful ten-yard perfect touchdown pass to Taylor, giving the 49ers the lead. Taylor's only catch of the game. Rice played the perfect decoy. He acted "as well as Denzel Washington," he would later claim. Pandemonium reigned on the field.

San Francisco's defense still had to step it up, however, just like six years ago against Dallas, to ensure the victory. Boomer Esiason's final pass to Chris Collinsworth was broken up. The final seconds slipped off the scoreboard like raindrops down a windshield after the storm.

The 49ers celebrated their third Super Bowl of the eighties. The dynasty rolled.

After the game, we cornered R. C. who had a lot going on.

"Tell us. Tell us," we begged like little kids. "Explain what happened on that final dramatic play."

R. C. sighed and talked to us as a teacher addressed school kids at recess. "A 20 Halfback Curl X-Up."

"What's that mean?"

"Using Rice as the decoy, Roger Craig became the primary receiver on a curl-up."

"We always called it a button hook," I said, "but what happened wrong?"

"Both backs lined up in the wrong positions, son. Didn't you notice?"

Here we go again. I'll never see the game at their level. Why rub it in?

"The Niner running backs," R. C. explained to us little kids, "Roger Craig and Tom Rathman, in all the confusion, lined up in each other's position, on the wrong sides. It happens.

"Joe spotted this. He knew once set, they couldn't change their positions, and being cool about it, man, Joe go with the play anyway. Tom Rathman, he be hearin' Joe's signals, realized he was in Craig's position. Since this *position* was the primary receiver, he ran the route.

"Roger Craig figured Rathman would stay home and protect Joe's ass from a blitz, and since the play was essentially *for* him, he also ran the route. Since both backs ran the same route, they canceled each other out, you see? They were easily covered and nearly ran into each other and attracted a crowd. Montana should've gotten creamed. Any other QB would have."

Someone called R. C., and the big guy ran off.

I later learned that Joe, after seeing Craig was easily covered, reacted quickly and decided on the world's largest stage to quickly look for his number 2 option, John Taylor, who, as I said, had not had a pass thrown his way all day. In fact, Taylor was seldom a target. He had snagged only twenty-three passes total in his two years thus far as a 9er. Not a lot of experience to be a target in a do-or-die situation. But then again, no one expected it.

He *was* open, but only barely. It'd take the perfect pass. Taylor had but a slight half-step on his defender. Of course, Joe Cool simply rifled the Super Bowl–winning strike into a windshield with the wipers on, ripping out the heart of Cincinnati.

It would forever be known in Forty-Niner folklore as *The Drive*. Copy and paste the URL below to check it out.[37]

Montana had just orchestrated an eleven-play, ninety-two-yard drive to score the winning touchdown. Ninety-two yards! The man started the drive with the John Candy incident and performed throughout the drive as if he had ice water pumping through his vein's sans the hyperventilating moment.

Joe surgically cut through the Bengal's committed defense *en route* to scoring the winning touchdown while steering a masterful strategy by the sly Silver Fox, Coach Walsh.

Walsh said in the postgame interview: "There's only one thing to say about Joe Montana.[38] He's the best there is and the best there ever was. Period."

Jerry Rice, the Super Bowl MVP, went from 49ers star to 49ers legend with 11 receptions, 215 receiving yards, a Super Bowl record, and clutch, clutch catches.

Of course, they easily could have given the MVP to Joe if he hadn't already won several Super Bowl MVPs. Joe threw a stunning 357 yards, mostly in the second half, and engineered the most famous game-ending drive of all time.

It was the triumphant end of an era. It was the mountaintop, the pinnacle for a team of good guys, their magnum opus, a team that did

---

37   The Drive: https://www.youtube.com/watch?v=SrcPy3HiiUk

38   On February 5, 2017, Tom Brady won his fifth Super Bowl ring, engineering an improbable comeback to match Joe Montana's against the Bengals. But then he lost against the Eagles on February 2, 2018 even though The Pats were heavily favored. So the great debate continues as to whom the greatest quarterback in history is now. The answer? Whichever team you root for. New England fans have their rationale for sure. However, in the Super Bowl where the lights shine the brightest on the greatest, Niner Nation has the following three facts to keep Joe squarely in the conversation for GOAT. Number 1, passer rating: Brady 95.3, Montana, 127.8 (which is beyond incredible). Number 2, interceptions: Brady 5, Montana 0. Number 3, losses: Brady 3, Montana 0.

things the right way, going against adversity once again to become Super Bowl champions.

After the game, Coach Walsh knew something no one else did. Sam Wyche, his former brother-in-arms, not only ran across the crowded field to congratulate his former mentor but ended up helping him off the field. Sam placed his arm around him in a touching show of good sportsmanship. Coach Walsh was that overcome with emotion. When was the last time you saw the losing coach help the winning coach off the field?

Here's why. Coach Walsh, immediately afterward, shocked everyone in San Francisco and inside the NFL down to their dental fillings.

He retired.

What? Why? Not only were the 49ers at their *zenith* but also were equipped with the most valuable of lessons: knowing and *feeling* what happens when you get too cocky and overconfident. The Niners would never allow that to happen again.

He *should never* have retired. He was still vibrant and relevant.

Pete Rozelle also retired as the NFL commissioner, and the entire security system at San Francisco and Burns Security changed: more real professionals coming in and more of us amateurs going out.

Flying out of Miami, looking out my airplane window at the low giant cloud formations, beyond tired from the late-night revelry, I realized this was the end of an era. It was as if I read the final page, pulled the bookmark out, closed the book, held it tightly to my chest, and gave it one last hug. I stared at cloud formations I had never seen before, and they were terrific. I joined one and drifted off into a deep REM, stage IV slumber.

Newly married, my wife, Maureen, pregnant, I would have a son named Ricky in a few months. My corporate job of regional vice president of the western region meant I'd be flying into different western cities constantly. With my new family, I found a new way to spend my Sundays, which was all this Niner gig was ever was supposed to be.

As noted earlier, growing up as a kid loving sports on the East Coast, rooting for the NY Giants, never a one time did I see the Giants make a single playoff game, live or on television. Then I moved to the Bay

Area and counting the Oakland Ray-Duz, I went or watched six San Francisco Bay Area Super Bowls within a nine-year span. Unbelievable really. Six Super bowls in nine years. Such good luck, really—for a change.

EPILOGUE

1989

THE FOLLOWING YEAR, the Team of the Eighties, The San Francisco Forty-Effin-Niners, still peaking, ran at full efficiency throughout the league like a locomotive running down the track through pillows. They tore through the league like the Berliners tore through the Wall on November 9 of that same year.

On October 17, 1989, the Loma Prieta earthquake struck the Bay Area, registering a jaw-dropping 7.1 on the Richter scale. Although concrete chunks of Candlestick fell during Game 3 of the World Series, the unique architectural design of the grand old ballpark was credited with saving thousands of lives. The City burnt from flames. Both the Nimitz freeway and the Bay Bridge experienced collapses, costing lives. Officials postponed the World Series. Houses, including Joe DiMaggio's in the expensive Marina District, crumbled. The devastation spread everywhere.

Yet, as I said earlier, Candlestick stood tall, protecting all. Formed into sections that literally rolled left to right, rather than falling, the Stick had no casualties nor problems. The 49ers moved their game on Sunday, October 22, to Stanford Stadium defeating the New England Patriots 37–20. They dedicated the game exclusively to their shaken fans.

New coach George Seifert, Coach Walsh's former defensive coordinator, was most wise. To his complete and utter credit, he did not change a thing. The 49ers finished the 1989 regular season with a league-best 14-and-2 record. They cruised on all cylinders straight into the playoffs.

Round 1: they obliterated The Minnesota Vikings yet again 41–13, eliminating them from the playoffs for the second year in a row by a wide margin, settling that score.

Round 2: they creamed their rivals, the LA Rams, 30–3 to win the NFC Championship.

Super Bowl XXIV: a national audience witnessed the biggest beat down *ever* administered to a team in the Super Bowl. San Francisco kicked the living daylights out of the John Elway–led Denver Broncos 55–10 and created forty—count them, forty—new Super Bowl records in this one single game. It was utter destruction. Even at this late date, this game remains as the most lopsided victory in Super Bowl history.

Joe Montana, after years under Walsh's tutelage and now the de facto leader of the entire team, stepped up. He had the best season of his career and was the consensus Player of the Year.

Montana's 112.4 quarterback rating smashed the previous NFL single-season record. Joe picked up his third Super Bowl MVP and threw five—yes, five— touchdown passes in the big game.[39]

In my humble opinion, Joe would not have become such a legend had Walsh not benched and humbled him against Minnesota three years ago or if Walsh hadn't *challenged* Joe's starting position two years ago by using Steve Young to push Joe's competitive juices.

Steve—you had to hand it to him—handled all this with grace and dignity. Eventually, Mr. Young also earned *his* Super Bowl ring as the game's MVP in 1994 as well and went on to a fabulous Hall of Fame career. During his 1994 MVP campaign, he set a new NFL season record for passer rating at 112.8.

Joe owned four Super Bowl rings, had his most productive games ever in his career on the biggest stage, and—get this—he never threw a single interception in four Super Bowls. Perfection to the *T*. He evolved from being in discussions as one of the greatest football players of all time to being one of the greatest *athletes* of all time.

In fact, the following season, 1990, they finished 14–2 yet again. They had the lead against the New York Giants and had matters under control in the NFC title game. Suddenly, out of nowhere, unexpectedly, Father Time snuck up on Joe when he wasn't looking.

---

39   His overall Super Bowl quarterback rating of 127.83 is—as of this writing in 2018—still tops all time by far.

Just when it inevitably looked like another Montana Super Bowl was on the horizon, a third in a row, well, like the first time you saw the Beatles on *Ed Sullivan*, you would never forget where you were when the moment occurred. I sat on a bar stool with a great German friend called Bild, watching TV in a Penn State bar, having watched a Nittany Lion victory the night before at Beaver Stadium. Joe got smashed in the back, his blind side, so hard by a rushing New York Giant, Leonard Marshall, that Joe literally disappeared from the TV screen.

"Montana back to pass, rolls right, *wham*, gone."

Montana suffered a bruised sternum, bruised stomach, cracked ribs, a broken hand, a broken finger and a severe concussion. With no Joe, the shocked Niners immediately fell apart and lost a game they figuratively had in the bag.

Joe missed the following entire 1991 season. When he returned in 1992, Steve Young was now firmly, finally, and fully in control. He was having an incredible season and becoming the league's MVP, his first of two that wrapped up Joe's spectacular career with San Francisco. I'm forever grateful and humbled I witnessed it.

Joe left behind an immortal legacy. He threw for over 40,000 yards, won four Super Bowls, and still holds the record with pass attempts—122—without an interception.

Hell, San Francisco traded Joe to the Kansas City Chiefs at the very end of his career, making room for his heir apparent, Steve Young. Joe, utilizing his amazing leadership skills, which cannot be measured by numbers, *still* led his new team to the AFC Championship game. And this on a team that hadn't won a playoff game since 1970 or, at that time, twenty-three years ago! He even defeated the 49ers 24–17 in the regular season against Steve Young to prove a point. Joe's two TD passes matched Young's interception total. Joe retired soon afterward, going out on top.

Watching Joe's peak years up close was a phenomenal experience during my security guard career. But it wasn't just Joe. At one time or another, I got to pound a shoulder pad and say, "Good luck today" to Ronnie Lott, the greatest safety ever; to Jerry Freaking Rice, definitely the best wide receiver ever; Randy Cross and Dwight Clark;

Coach Walsh (no, he wasn't wearing pads); Roger Craig; tight end extraordinares Brent Jones and later Russell Francis; my main man, R. C. Owens; Fred Dean-fense; Eric Wright and more. Best of all, without a doubt was the *feeling* of that Forty-Niner team spirit when it soared. I still get a rush reminiscing about it.

Even though I was a mere peon, a brokenhearted part-time security guard, I would not trade those *rich* experiences from being behind the scenes of the Team of the Eighties for all the San Francisco gold in Fort Knox.

The San Francisco Forty-Niners won seven out of ten NFC Championships that decade and earned the title *the Team of the Eighties*. However, quick side note, their 113 victories were more than any other team in the *nineties* as well. That's ten more wins than second-place Buffalo and twelve more than Dallas. Thus, their dynasty covered two consecutive decades.

In conclusion, much like the Golden Gate Bridge, the golden Niner helmets or the original 1849er miners panning for gold, the 1980s, looking back, those truly were the Golden years.

During my first year of retirement—if you could refer to it that way since it was a seasonal part-time job—I went ahead and visited El Capitán during a game I finally *paid* to enter. I never officially said goodbye so figured why not?

As usual, he sat enshrouded in a cloud of smoke inside his office. "Hello, El Capitán. You were right guaranteeing the 49ers would go all the way last year. You should've bet. You could've made a ton of money."

He presented his sinister smile. "Who said I didn't?" Smoke just naturally drifted out of his mouth even when he wasn't smoking.

"Hmmm, interesting." As always, he looked busy shuffling through papers at his desk, so I just blurted it out, "Please, El Capitán, sir, one final question, and I'll split."

He looked up. I thought he'd say, "You can call me by my real name now." He didn't.

"I've always wondered about one thing. Now, I can finally put this behind me. It's always bothered me. I'll take you into my confidence, and you know you can trust me. You still do trust me, right?"

"I do."

"Please, the man in the dumpster, El Capitán—and I'll not say another word—was he dead or alive?"

"What guy?"

"The fan we found lying in the dumpster. Remember how he was famously clutching his bottle of beer?"

"I don't recollect seeing anything like that."

"C'mon. *You* didn't see him, but you heard about him. The guy in the green army surplus jacket clutching his beer bottle. Remember? People were astonished he never let go of the bottle. Witnessed by the SFPD and dozens of fans. That guy."

"I know nothing about it." He looked at me with as expressionless of a face as a house cat. He got up, extended his skeletal arm, and grinned only out of one side of his mouth.

"You sonovabitch," I said, shaking his hand and my head at the same time.

ABOUT THE AUTHOR

MY NAME IS Rick Pucci, Sr. I grew up in a middle-class home in northeast Pennsylvania in small-town Glen Lyon/ Nanticoke. Our family included five children, two parents (Rick and Jeri), my Godmother (Tina), a dog and various inhabitants of our back-yard including a full-blown chicken coop. We had a dozen rows of tomato plants and also five full barrels of wine in our basement from our three massive grapevines. None of this was uncommon among the Italian-American families in the area. Baby boomer kids like me poured into the streets for games and sports, but our town was reliant on coal and soon suffered greatly on the socio-economic spectrum. Jobs became scarce.

I caught a lucky break. A local star football coach named Al Cihocki got me a chance for a full football scholarship, and amazingly I passed the try-outs. I thought I would become the next great linebacker at football power Penn State. Such a laughable plan in hindsight, considering I stood only six feet tall, weighed 185 pounds, and lacked speed.

A sophomore year injury saved me from four years on the bench, a proverbial blessing in disguise that released me to the wondrous Penn State way-of-life. I met a young lady on campus (Joanne), and after graduating, we relocated to the sunny climes of the San Francisco Bay Area where I continued my education at the affordable San Jose State University graduate program and started a career in finance.

Then she dumped me. I needed something to keep my mind off a broken heart, especially on Sundays, so I took a part-time security job for 7 bucks-an-hour at perhaps the worst franchise in all of sports at that time, The Forty Effin Niners.

Landing that job was miracle enough, but then the Niners proceeded to win 7 divisional crowns and 4 Super Bowls during my 8 seasons with the organization. Throughout this period, I took copious notes and up-close photographs. At both my universities, my favorite courses, English writing and Composition came in mighty handy.

As President and founder of my own company, Park Ridge Financial, Inc., I write all the time, believing in the adage coined by Edward Bulwer-Lytton that "The Pen is Mightier than the sword." I also attended writing workshops at Evanston Writers Workshop (EWW), Jerry Cleaver's Immediate Fiction classes, and currently Story Studio in Chicago.

On a personal note, the greatest book I've ever read, bar none, is Irving Stone's *the Agony and The Ecstasy*. It changed my life. It's a bio on one of my heroes, Michelangelo Buonarroti, who wrote, "Man Gains his greatest strengths through periods of adversity." All his greatest works such as The Pietà, The David, and The Sistine Chapel came during stressful times.

Having established a successful business (where I no longer have to put in those incalculable hours), and after putting two kids, Ricky and Scarlett through Master's Degree Programs, I finally found the time to write. Then, in 2018, I lost my beloved wife Maureen of 33 years, whom I adored, to a rare cancer. So I am practicing what Michelangelo preached, pouring my energy and grief into writing. I'm also donating proceeds from the sales of this book towards detecting biliary cancer, which is what took away my soulmate. I hope you enjoy my crazy accidental memoir from the Niners days. Meanwhile, my new novel, *Peaceful Violence*, is already "in the can." Look for it in bookstores or online soon.